The Executive Résumé Book

Loretta D. Foxman

John Wiley & Sons, Inc.

New York ◆ Chichester ◆ Brisbane ◆ Toronto ◆ Singapore

OTHER CAREER BOOKS FROM WILEY

The Complete Q & A Job Interview Book, Jeffrey B. Allen
The Five Minute Interview, Richard H. Beatty
Job Search: The Total System, Kenneth Dawson and Sheryl N. Dawson
CareerMap: Deciding What You Want, Getting It, and Keeping It!, Neil Yeager
Revising Your Resume, Nancy Schuman and William Lewis

Publisher: Stephen Kippur
Editor: Katherine Schowalter
Managing Editor: Corinne McCormick
Editing, Design, and Production: Publications Development Company of Crockett, Texas.

The Foreword writer's views do not necessarily represent the views of his employer.

This publication is designed to provide accurate and authoritative information in regard to the subject matter covered. It is sold with the understanding that the publisher is not engaged in rendering legal, accounting, or other professional service. If legal advice or other expert assistance is required, the services of a competent professional person should be sought. FROM A DECLARATION OF PRINCIPLES JOINTLY ADOPTED BY A COMMITTEE OF THE AMERICAN BAR ASSOCIATION AND A COMMITTEE OF PUBLISHERS.

Copyright © 1989 by John Wiley & Sons, Inc.

All rights reserved. Published simultaneously in Canada.

Reproduction or translation of any part of this work beyond that permitted by section 107 or 108 of the 1976 United States Copyright Act without the permission of the copyright owner is unlawful. Requests for permission or further information should be addressed to the Permission Department, John Wiley & Sons, Inc.

Library of Congress Cataloging-in-Publication Data

Foxman, L. D. (Loretta D.)
The executive résumé book / Loretta Foxman.
p. cm.
Bibliography: p. 203
ISBN 0-471-60633-2. ISBN 0-471-60634-0 (pbk.)
1. Résumés (Employment) 2. Job hunting. 3. Executives.
4. Professions. I. Title.
HF5383.F818 1989
658.4'09—dc19 88-30588
CIP

Printed in the United States of America

20 19 18 17 16 15 14 13

To my mother, Helen Foxman,
heroine and coach.
She taught me about strategy and achieving.
And to Ann Polsky, my mother-in-law,
friend and cheering section.
Her definitions of ethics and integrity
are to be emulated.

Foreword

Sometimes, the decision to pursue another job comes by chance. More often, it is when the challenge of your current job begins to fade and you begin glancing at the want ads. But once in a career, it can just happen. A slam on the side of the head. A merger. A restructuring. New management. The result is always the same: devastating . . . at first. But once you deal with the emotional aspects, you can actually view this period of your life as useful, motivating, and even memorable. With luck, it will be brief. Hopefully, it will be relatively painless. With this book, it can be made a lot easier.

The résumé, of course, is where everyone's journey begins. But, to too many people it is simply a required document that moves you from one point A to point B. The author of this book positions it as much more; as part of a strategic plan. Loretta Foxman has researched not only various aspects of what ought to go into a résumé, but also what shouldn't. She has investigated the do's and the don'ts; the why's and the wherefore's; the turn ons and the turnoffs. She then gives examples. She positions the résumé as a strategic tool in a fully stocked arsenal.

Ironically, the most professional manager, one who painstakingly builds a highly motivated team for himself, becomes deaf, dumb, and blind to those very same qualifications when the tables are turned. The executive who successfully challenged his own people to cut expenses neglects to identify a 20 percent cost reduction as an accomplishment on his own résumé. And the manager who didn't make the cut when a new management team came to town fails to see a silver lining because he is too close to the forest to see the trees.

The author has spent her career working with executives—human resource professionals, headhunters, CEOs, and those of us who at one time or another were "just passing through." Her effort here is well conceived, well documented, and provides a welcome reassurance.

EDWARD F. HERBERT
Director of Communications
MCI Telecommunications Corporation

Preface

"Winning isn't everything. It's the only thing."
Vince Lombardi

To be a major player in the executive job search game, you need a strategic approach. The *Executive Résumé Book* will help you to take action so that you can put your résumé on paper and get the job offer you want. You will learn strategies that will help you play and win the job search game. Your objective? To get the position you want—that's winning the game.

This book is for you whether you are a senior executive, mid-level manager, or a professional. With carefully developed strategies, you will learn to cope with the rigorous standards a senior executive faces in the job search process. Businesses use strategic thinking to formulate a business plan; you must also use a strategic plan to be successful. This book will help you to develop the skills you need to play smart and get the job you want.

"The Executive Game Plan" presented in this book is a proven and tested set of strategies developed by my outplacement firm. My clients tell me that these strategies work and that they are finding better opportunities and compensation levels in a highly competitive executive job market.

Another outstanding feature of this book is the executive résumé survey. I interviewed executive recruiters and employers—those making the screening decisions. I have validated and clarified what is presently known about the expectations of executive recruiters, corporate recruiters, human resource professionals, and general management officers. In the survey, which was given to a nation-wide cross-section of companies and industries, I asked these professionals important questions relating to the job selection process. Their responses, some of which are surprising and go against what has been assumed as accepted practice, are found in Chapter 4. As far as I know, no other résumé book contains this type of information. A combination of the survey results and the specific winning strategies will give you the tools you need to write a winning résumé, gain that competitive edge, and conduct a winning job-search campaign.

This book is divided into two parts. The first part tells you what to do and the second part shows you how to do it. We have used case histories and quotes from real people extensively. Although all names in the case histories have been changed, the circumstances and situations are ones that have actually occurred and ones that we believe will help you through your own "situations."

The quotes are directly from the interviews conducted in the research for this book. They will help you use the "cross over strategy" that we discuss in Chapter 3.

PART 1 THE EXECUTIVE GAME PLAN: THE RÉSUMÉ

Because this book contains inside job information from potential employers, the serious executive job seekers will put it on their "invaluable" list. This information is provided by the survey participants and reveals what employers want. Having this information enables you to build the best résumé possible.

Constructing the résumé is a step-by-step process. This process is explained to you clearly and concisely. Mechanics, content, and style are fully demonstrated, and sample résumés are given as examples.

You will also learn a technique for changing places with prospective employers in order to understand what they want. This is called the *Cross Over (the Desk) Strategy*. In other words, your mind crosses over to the employer's side of the desk; you learn to put yourself in his or her shoes to understand what that person wants and needs.

PART 2 THE EXECUTIVE GAME PLAN: GETTING THE JOB

In Part 2, you will learn how to plan and play the job-hunting game with skill and finesse. You will be guided through each remaining step as you climb to success.

Now that you have the résumé, you will learn how to use it to your best advantage. You will learn about smart tools and techniques, such as letters that work for you, telephone skills that market you, interviewing techniques that close the sale for you, and strategies and guidelines that make the job search easier for you. You will learn the best ways to reach and develop your contacts, how to respond to ads, and how to find and use organizations and reference books that can get you the job offer you are seeking.

If you still need assistance after you finish this book, refer to Chapter 10 for a list of sources. Each source is evaluated so that you can decide which ones are best for you. Also included is a bibliography of other relevant reading material.

SUMMARY OF STRATEGIES

1. Get yourself ready, get set, get organized!
2. Know what you want to do—then do it. Make straight for your goal and go undefeated in spirit to the end.
3. The reader of the résumé—the customer—is asking, "What can you do for me?"

4. Transmit only what your customer wants to receive (hear or see).
5. Continually cross over the desk and step into the shoes of your potential employer.
6. Use your résumé as little as possible—only when you must!
7. Know thyself.
8. Pay attention to the smallest detail. Even a misplaced word can be detrimental.
9. Let your accomplishments rather than your zeal to be noticed set your résumé apart.
10. Use the other formats only when the chronological does not work for you.
11. Manage the ways you use your résumé with the same diligence you used to develop it.
12. Send everyone who helps you a thank you letter, even if their help was minimal.
13. Keeping score will get you there more quickly.
14. The more you use the telephone, the easier it will be.
15. Learn to make the interviewer's job easier.
16. The more creative you are in using all available resources, the more effective you will be.
17. It is foolish to try to conduct a job search without professional guidance.

ACKNOWLEDGMENTS

This book began with my first outplacement client many years ago. He was a president and chief operating officer who found himself in the throes of an unplanned job search due to a restructuring within his former company. I am certain I learned as much from him as he learned from me. The challenges for the highest achievers, the senior level job seekers, are more complex and sometimes tougher. I am indebted to this first client as well as all those who followed.

Judy Bates, President of Data Details, stayed with me, helping to refine and structure the final edit. Her word processing support went beyond the domain of simple data input. She edited, counseled, and cheered. She worked through the night at the end to meet an impossible deadline. I thank you wholeheartedly, Judy.

My editor and production editor Katherine Schowalter and Nancy Land respectively, remained faithful to this project through drafts and edits and extended deadlines. They knew I would do it and maybe just because of their limitless patience, I did.

Thank you to Walter Polsky, my first mentor, my talented business partner, and, best of all, my husband, who spent many days, evenings, and weekends discussing, hypothesizing, strategizing, and, of course, editing.

The staff of the Cambridge Human Resource Group gave their creative ideas and unmatched patience and energy in support of this project. The research survey, the inordinate amount of staff time, and the coming through when there seemed to be no answers to meeting a crushing deadline are humbly appreciated. To Norma Noesen, Judy O'Brien, Pamela Pickett, Maureen Hawkins, Shawna Reed, and Sona Iyengar, I give my respect and appreciation.

Nick Podoba, Corporate Director of Human Resources at International Minerals and Chemicals, deserves more than a simple thank you. He was the catalyst for a redesign of the research survey. He initiated a taskforce to refine the survey input query. His contribution to the integrity of this book has not gone unnoticed.

Aside from the 163 survey respondents who took time out from their busy work schedules to make an important contribution to this book, I want to thank M. Catherine Fleming, Ph.D, Judy Strauss, Ph.D., and Joyce Watts who worked on the research survey design and development, and Lynda Foxman who also helped with the research survey and project management. My thanks.

Finally, there is Judy Rosemarin, a director of the Career Continuation program at the Chemical Bank in New York who deserves my appreciation for diligently reading that first draft.

Contents

Part 1

The Executive Game Plan: The Résumé

1

What Is This Game All About?

Business is a game: the greatest game in the world if you know how to play it.

Thomas J. Watson
Former CEO of IBM

WHY AN EXECUTIVE RÉSUMÉ GAME PLAN?

> Just as a strategic business plan helps a business run more effectively, a strategic résumé plan helps a résumé work more successfully.

As an outplacement and career-management consultant, I have worked with countless job-hunting executives, managers, and professionals. Often, a new client walks into my office and wants a résumé completed by the end of the day.

I always tell them, "Rome was not built in a day; neither should your résumé be. If the résumé is going to be a winner, there must be a game plan. It will be competing with hundreds of résumés for the chance at a choice interview. You can't afford to throw something together in haste and expect it to work effectively."

Typically, the client grinds his or her teeth and tries to humor me through the most difficult and frustrating part of the job-search campaign. Although the client is impatient, I must stress that the résumé requires hard work. Writing a résumé is the most exhausting part of the job search. If done correctly, it takes time—sometimes as much as a week—to prepare a final draft. People tend to feel impatient about this process. It tends to feel entirely too passive.

An executive would not be allowed to start a new business for a company without a well-planned strategy to make it successful. Yet, day after day, I see men and women who think they can wing it through the job search with a last minute résumé. What typically emerges is a laundry list of jobs, responsibilities, and achievements, but not always a résumé that will make it in the tough competitive executive and professional job market?

Again, executive thinking is strategic thinking. *Planning and directing a series of actions is the best way to reach a specific goal.* If you are going after an executive job, your résumé must demonstrate your capabilities, including your ability to think strategically. Otherwise, you could find yourself in the same predicament as John Milano in the following case history:

> John Milano [name changed as are all names in case histories cited in this book] was referred to me and called to ask my help. "What's your problem?" I asked. "I left my position five months ago as the chief financial officer of a consumer electronics firm," he said. "I have read numerous books on the job search. I still do not have a job. Frankly, I'm not sure what to believe. Almost every time I read a book, I change my résumé."

A 10-minute conversation with this executive told me he was floundering. With no preplanned course of action, he had floated for months. He tried to discover the techniques on his own by using as many self-help books as he could find. His problem, however, was that he had no strategic plan for staying on target in his job search.

Many people go to bookstores and libraries for help in preparing a résumé. There they find an excess of information and mixed advice. At last count, there were 40 résumé books in the latest list of *Books in Print*. Of these, 15 were targeted to specific professions or groups, such as nurses, technicians, women, paralegals, and so on. In addition, résumé sections are found in almost every job-search book written. Good advice is available, but it is not always the right advice for a specific situation.

Very little has been written for the senior executive, who faces rigorous challenges in launching a job search. The advice for more senior executives found within these pages is the best source of information for professionals and managers as well. This book is a benchmark for all jobseekers because it adheres to these high level standards.

This book will review the good, the bad, and the conflicting do's and don'ts that have been expounded on by career gurus over the last four decades. What is the prevailing advice? Who are the "customers" making hiring decisions? What does the employer really want? These questions will all be answered.

Strategic thinking about yourself and your career is not easy. Nor is it easy to write a résumé that demonstrates your strategic thinking. But the potential payoffs—more interviews, a shorter job search, and a more satisfying position—are well worth the effort. Often, the results are revealing and encouraging.

> Valerie Moses, a marketing vice president, balked at doing the strategic thinking and hard work necessary to develop her executive résumé. "I don't want to spend the time," she stated. "Plus, I've got a résumé that worked for me seven years ago, so all I need to do is update it."
>
> "Trust me on this one," I counseled her. "It is a lot of work, but the result will be worth the effort." She followed the game plan in this book and returned to my office to confide, "My goodness, they weren't paying me enough!"

The hardest part of tackling anything new, such as writing a résumé, is getting started, deciding where to start, and how to go about it. That's where this book comes in. It helps you develop a game plan and specific strategies.

To help you write the best résumé *for you*—a successful résumé—a cross-section of organizations across the country has been surveyed. These executives, hiring managers, executive recruiters, and outplacement consultants were asked what employers really want. The results are incorporated into this book—the best strategies for the most effective résumé. Make this information work for you. Don't be fooled by the idea that you can get lucky.

Just looking at the typical itinerary a résumé faces as it winds its way into the reader's hands and mind will vividly emphasize how important this document really is.

9:10 A.M. The résumé reaches its destination by mail.

10:20 A.M. It is sorted in the company mailroom.

11:57 A.M.	The documentation of your existence is delivered to the addressee.
6:13 P.M.	Your résumé, along with two more inches of résumés and/or paperwork, are stuffed into the recipient's briefcase.
6:35 P.M.	It's Thursday and he is tired; he reads the newspaper instead of your résumé on his train ride home.
8:00 P.M.	Friday evening and your résumé sits in his briefcase unread. He had good intentions for Thursday night. Friday evening is fleeting.
Saturday (all day)	Your résumé and everything else in his briefcase are ignored again.
Sunday 2:20 P.M.	The dog is barking, his wife wants to know why he has to work; after all, this is the weekend. His son wants a ride to the movies. The in-laws are coming to dinner. The lawn needs mowing.
Sunday 3:15 P.M.	The recruiter has Sunday afternoon obligations on his mind and this stack of résumés (yours included) under his eyes.
Sunday 5:10 P.M.	He is racing through—a quick perusal—that's all your résumé gets. True, not every résumé reader has all these distractions to deal with. However, getting through that stack of résumés at high speed is paramount.
At any time	Will yours be selected for the "These look good" stack . . . and subsequently for the "I want to talk to this candidate" pile?

If your résumé is not absolutely clear, the résumé reader (the recruiter, the hiring manager) will get a confusing and often frustrating message. Consider the résumé reading workload recruiters face:

Michael Mills places an ad in the Sunday *New York Times* and the Tuesday *Wall Street Journal* almost every week to recruit a variety of professional and management level candidates. Some weeks he advertises for one or two; often he runs ads for as many as five positions. He receives from 100 to 500 responses to each ad for a weekly total of as many as 6000 résumés. His employer, a Big 8 public accounting firm, typically has him working on 20 to 25 openings at one time, and he screens résumés for all of them.

Katherine Curant is the manager of professional recruitment for a Midwest middle market bank. Her recruiting responsibilities are not even close to Mills' volume. She sees 300 to 500 résumés a month even when she is *not* running an ad, because all unsolicited résumés are routed to her. Unlike some personnel people, she personally reviews every résumé that comes into the bank.

Your résumé is the key that can unlock the interview door. If it is only a cursory list of your prior positions, responsibilities, and accomplishments, its chances of getting into the "to be interviewed" pile are minimal. Unless your accomplishments are hinged on a *market-driven approach*, your résumé could be weak and ineffectual. If you follow the advice in this book, you can increase your chances of hitting the "to be interviewed" pile.

Whether you are a senior executive or a middle manager, you face a particularly challenging job-search campaign. It is estimated that more than 100,000 upper-level and mid-level management and executive positions were eliminated by downsizing, mergers, and acquisitions in the late 1980s, and there seems to be no relief in sight. The executive who has a job today may be out of work tomorrow through no fault of his or her own.

It makes good business sense to keep an up-to-date résumé. That résumé is even better if it has been carefully written using a professional and strategic approach.

The choice is yours. You can slide through your job search, and unless you are very lucky, you will waste time and effort only to end up with a mediocre job. Alternatively, you can use this book to learn what employers want in a résumé and how to implement strategies and techniques to enhance your campaign. The trained and knowledgeable job seeker gets a better job in less time—as much as 80 percent faster than the person who tries to do it all alone without professional guidance.

This book will help you cut through the job-search maze with a crystal clear résumé that is targeted to your personal goals and desired job market. You might be looking for a senior executive, junior executive, or professional position. In any case, when you finish studying these carefully developed chapters, you will be the strategist; the expert. Just as in playing chess, your strategy wins the game. The difference in the job-search game is that it affects your life, your family, your happiness, and your future.

RÉSUMÉ STRESS IS TO BE EXPECTED—IT MIGHT EVEN HELP

Even the most intelligent person is often uncomfortable with writing a résumé. The hard work, the time required, and the committed effort needed create anxiety. Even more alarming is the knowledge that this document may disqualify you from the game.

> Robert Randle started his own consulting practice eight years ago in Rochester, New York. He had no contacts and no experience owning his own business. After living there for six months, he took the plunge. Randle obtained a loan on his house, rented office space, and began his new business. Today, Randle has offices in three major cities and billings of nearly $2 million. When asked the reason for his success, he answered, "Fear . . . the best motivator."

Fear may not be the best of motivators; however, it is certainly an effective one. Randle used his fear. He had no clients, no contacts, and virtually no money other than the loan on his house. His wife didn't work and there were small children to consider. What chance did he have? He used his stress and anxiety to bring him success. He didn't allow obstacles to stand in his way. The job seeker can do the same.

Stress for the jobseeker can be large or small depending on who owns the particular fear and where that executive is at the moment:

- Is the search for a job a race of time (If I don't get out soon, I am going to be fired.)?
- Is the job loss very recent or has he or she been unemployed for an extended period?
- Is this too close to another major life trauma such as a divorce or a death?
- Is there a medical or other special problem in the family that requires the continued income?

Like Randle, the executive, looking for a job is faced with many unknowns from how to begin the job search to what is the most appropriate style for the résumé. Solid answers to these questions can alleviate the fear and stress related to the job search.

Relax and let's begin. The executive game plan will become one of the most rewarding experiences of your career. It may feel like hard work right now, but you can motivate yourself to continue your efforts. You will get results!

2

On Your Mark: Be One of the Highest Achievers

Everyone wants to win; but show me the person who is committed to organize and prepare to win and I'll show you a winner.

Bill Purcell
Head Coach, New York Giants

ARE YOUR DUCKS IN ORDER? IF NOT, GET ORGANIZED

▶ **Strategy 1:** Get yourself ready, get set, get organized!

The Olympic runner begins his personal race to first place months ahead of time; practicing with the appropriate diet, exercise, training, and commitment. Shortly before the race begins, he is open—receptive. His frame of mind flexes to win. His trainer counsels him about the connection between his attitude and winning. Some athletes have learned to use self-hypnosis to prepare themselves.

Like the Olympic runner, senior executives want to run and win. Leading experts like Warren Bennis, a nationally known consultant and professor contend that these winners (leaders and achievers) begin with a mindset. It is a constructive attitude that makes the difference. Get yourself *ready*:

- Forget about how you prepared your previous résumé(s). Open your perspective to what employers really want.
- Think about this intense effort (and it should be if you are doing it right) as laying the groundwork for an easier job search.
- Aim for superior quality. Your energies will reverberate throughout your campaign.

Get Yourself Organized

Gather all the written material you have, such as old résumés, journals, calendars, transcripts, and so on. These resources should be at your fingertips as you begin to prepare yourself for what is often called the most tedious part of the job search—the résumé.

GOAL DIRECTED: DEFINE AND FOCUS

Goals Definition: Position Objective

> While attending a cocktail reception of the Chicago chapter of Women in Management, (at the time, the majority of this group was in mid- to upper mid-management) I was standing with a group of people who were getting acquainted. A meeting was to follow, and it would be my first. I was not alone; there were many who were there for the first time. A woman walked up to our small group and said, "Hi, my name is Mary Bryant and I am looking for a job in management." My first reaction was surprise; my second was pleasure. I was surprised to see someone approach and be so forthright with a group of people she obviously didn't know. The group accepted the newcomer instantly, and no one appeared to be disturbed by the interruption. I stepped into my career-counseling shoes and began asking her questions: "What are you looking for? What have you done in previous positions? . . . " I kept coming back to the question of "What do you want?" and she kept responding with variations on the theme of "a position in management." I couldn't help her because she did not know what she wanted. I felt confused and frustrated. This is also how résumé readers feel when they encounter a résumé that is unspecific. Perhaps Mary Bryant is still looking for that vague and elusive position somewhere in management.

This case history illustrates the need for a clearly defined objective. It shows that you can deadend your résumé when you don't know where you are going. Just as you can't buy a bus ticket without having a destination in mind, neither can you find the job most suitable to you without knowing what you want.

An unclear objective is a quicker route into the circular file than you might think. Résumé screeners are busy people. Your entire career history, as well as your current goals and objectives, are represented by one or two pieces of paper containing an assortment of words. If these words are not clear and concise, your résumé doesn't stand a chance.

If your objective doesn't jump out and grab the reader's attention, there is little chance that these decision makers will take the time and energy necessary to reread your résumé. They won't try to figure out what your goals and objectives are. Instead, they will pass yours over and quickly find the résumés that are clear and concise.

The following exercises for defining your goals will help to simplify this phase of your job search.

Goals Definition: How to Set Job/Career Objectives

Instructions:

- Write a paragraph describing each of your career goals. If you have only one, that's fine. Write up to three objectives if you can. Then, number them from one to three in order of importance to you.
- Be sure to include the following information:

  Title and description

  Field/industry

  Function

  Company size

  Responsibilities

  Managing requirements (include the number of people you would like to manage)

  Growth potential

  Environment (even if it seems unimportant, for example, an office with a view)

Salary requirements

Location

- Be concise and specific.
- The Position Objective (see worksheet, p. 16) describes what you want in a job. It does not necessarily need to be stated on your résumé; it is probably best for most people to omit it from the résumé. (See section on contents in Chapter 6.)
- If naming the exact title of the job you want eludes you, write the best description you can.
- The goals worksheets (pp. 16–19) will help you determine whether and when you are ready to write a résumé.

Make sure you focus on one or two position objectives, but certainly no more than three. If your interests include more than three objectives, you are not ready to complete a résumé. If this is the case, it is necessary to do a personal and career assessment. There are excellent books and counselors who can help you. (See Chapter 10 and the Bibliography).

> Method goes far to prevent trouble in business, for it makes the task easy, hinders confusion, saves abundance of time, and instructs those who have business depending, what to do and what to hope.
>
> William Penn, 1694

The worksheet on p. 16 shows how to set up your career objective. The Rank space on the right can be used if you identify more than one objective.

As an example, consider a human resource executive who had two objectives. In the worksheet on p. 17, he listed each and then ranked them according to his preference.

Each of the following worksheets depicts another industry and will give you an insight on how to identify your objective regardless of your particular area, function, or industry.

GOALS DEFINITION WORKSHEET

Position Objective Rank ______

Title: ______

Field/Industry: ______

Function: ______

Company size: ______

Responsibilities: ______

______

______

______

Managing requirements: ______

Growth potential: ______

Environment: ______

Salary: ______

Location: ______

GOALS DEFINITION WORKSHEET

Position Objective Rank *1*

Title: *Vice President Human Resources*

Field/Industry: *Foods*

Function: *Human Resources*

Company size: *two billion (the larger the better)*

Responsibilities: *Direct all human resource activities for corporation. Report to CEO. Have impact on strategic planning.*

Managing requirements: *Staff of four to eight direct reports*

Growth potential: *to Senior V.P. Human Resources or move into administration.*

Environment: *Windows, view, close proximity to CEO*

Salary: *$135,000 + bonus*

Location: *Northeastern United States*

Position Objective Rank *2*

Title: *Consultant*

Field/Industry: *Not applicable*

Function: *Human Resource Consulting or Executive Search*

Company size: *Small—three to ten people*

Responsibilties: *Develop and manage external consulting projects for gamut of human resource issues*

Managing requirements: *Not important*

Growth potential: *Partner or principal*

Environment: *Team*

Salary: *Open*

Location: *Northeastern United States*

GOALS DEFINITION WORKSHEET

Position Objective Rank ______

Title: *Chief Financial Officer*

Field/Industry: *High Tech*

Function: *Finance*

Company size: *$350 million to $750 million*

Responsibilities: *Direct all controllership, tax, treasury and audit functions at corporate level*

Managing requirements: *Open. Number not important*

Growth potential: *Move to general management within five years.*

Environment: *Doesn't matter*

Salary: *$185,000 plus bonus and appropriate perks*

Location: *Open*

GOALS DEFINITION WORKSHEET

Position Objective Rank ______

Title: *Director of Communications*

Field/Industry: *Electronics/High Tech*

Function: *Public Relations*

Company size: *Fortune 1000*

Responsibilities: *Media relations, promotional programs, event planning*

Managing requirements: *Small staff (2–10)*

Growth potential: *Director of Public Relations*

Environment: *Creative, open*

Salary: *$80,000 to $90,000*

Location: *Not important*

Instructions for Job Goals

The worksheet on p. 21 is a long-range focusing exercise. It is designed as a process to help you think through your immediate and long-range career goals. This exercise should be analyzed and reworked at least once a year.

The steps to getting the job you want should be clear, concise, and specific. For example, if your immediate goal is a position that requires international exposure, you will want to identify the necessary steps required to obtain that position. Each of these steps can be further broken down into even smaller steps, for example:

- Develop a target list of companies that have international operations.
- Research what departments or units of the organizations that interest you are engaged in international activities.
- Identify what jobs in that unit would be viable for your present skill level.
- Do this with every potential position in the international business unit(s) of the company.
- Research and list appropriate contacts to network for openings and new contacts.
- If you are lacking skills or credentials, devise a plan to get the experience. Go back to school, do independent research, find a mentor, or do whatever else is necessary to reach your objective. The more senior your level, the less likely you are to need additional schooling. Still, it is a good idea to look at all your options.

This chapter was designed to teach you the skills you need to define and shape your goals. When your goals are defined in clear, concise, and measurable terms, you move from fantasizing about your dream job to being able to take the steps to make it a reality. The five rules on page 22 will serve as a quick review whenever you are faced with defining your career direction.

JOB GOALS WORKSHEET

Write your first choice position objective from the previous exercise: Goals Definition Worksheet.

Fill out a plan, such as the one below to cover the next 10 years. Even if you are unable to fill in all the blanks, the process will get you into a strategic planning mode. This will be of benefit not only for your immediate job goal, but also for all the ones to follow.

Job Goal Goal (Immediate)	What to Do to Get There	Time Frame
The job I want most within 6 mos: *Vice president marketing*	Means or Steps 1. 2. 3. 4. 5.	Completion Date: 1. 2. 3. 4. 5.
Job Goal (Near Term)	What to Do to Get There	Time Frame
The job I want in 2 years is: *Corporate vice president marketing—international*	Means or Steps 1. 2. 3. 4. 5.	Completion Date: 1. 2. 3. 4. 5.
Job Goal (Long Range)	What to Do to Get There	Time Frame
The job I want in 10 years is: *Executive vice president/ general management*	Means or Steps 1. 2. 3. 4. 5.	Completion Date: 1. 2. 3. 4. 5.

1. In specific terminology, state your objective in one or two sentences (a good test of your readiness for beginning your job search in earnest).
2. Be sure there is a definite time frame (two months, six months, or two years).
3. Break down your goal into the smallest action-steps possible (and add a time frame for each).
4. Establish your list of obstacles and steps for overcoming each one.
5. Continually ask yourself: Is this realistic? This goal? This action step? This obstacle?

The following strategy sums it up: Once you know what you want, write it down. Commit yourself to doing everything you can to get to your destination. When you are perfectly clear about where you are going, and when you can articulate that goal, the résumé reader can help you to reach your objective.

▸ **Strategy 2:** "Know what you want to do—then do it. Make straight for your goal and go undefeated in spirit to the end."

Ernestine Schumann-Hink

Knowing what you want is only half the equation. Without a true understanding of what the résumé screener wants, the résumé game is over. The next two chapters give fresh insight into what the résumé screener really wants from you and from your résumé.

3

The Cross Over (the Desk) Strategy

The difference between failure and success is doing a thing nearly right and doing a thing exactly right.

Edward Simmons

UNDERSTAND YOUR CUSTOMER

> Most executive recruiting is a response to a known problem. The more we feel an executive could handle "our" problems, the more likely we are to call him or her in.
>
> Susan Crowe
> Personnel Director,
> Abbott Laboratories
> North Chicago

A sale can rarely be made without an understanding of the customer and his needs. You want to sell yourself through your résumé, so you, too, must understand the needs of your "customers." Your customers are the résumé readers. Everyday you must sell your ideas both at home and at the office. You sell your boss on a new idea for moving a product through production more quickly. You sell your subordinates on the goals of a specific project. You sell your spouse on agreeing to go to the movie you have selected. Professional salespeople who have a high closing rate have refined the art of understanding the customer. They have developed this art into a highly sharpened skill. Understanding the basic needs, desires, insecurities, and personality style of the customer determines whether or not the sale is closed. The successful salesperson sells to the needs of the prospect.

Your résumé prepares the way for the most important sale you will make. The success of your résumé will ultimately affect not only your career, but your family and your future well-being.

Understanding your customer is "Basic Strategy 101" to the smart executive. Winning the executive job-search game is based on how well you know your customer—the résumé reader.

Do you understand who your customer is? The résumé plan, just like the business plan, must be based on what the customer wants. John F. Kennedy's adage, "Ask not what your country can do for you, but what you can do for your country," can be applied to the job-seeker. Simply substitute the word "company" for "country."

▶ **Strategy 3:** The reader of the résumé—the customer—is asking, "What can you do for me?"

The corner bakery wants the same things from its employees as the Fortune 500 companies do. They want to know what you can do for their companies, their clients, their customers, and for them personally. They want to know if job dedication and satisfaction is more important to you than company benefits. As they review your résumé, these decision makers are asking themselves all of the following questions:

- Can you improve productivity?
- Can you improve profits?
- Can you enhance services?
- Have you demonstrated, with hard facts, what you can do?
- Do you understand our business?
- Do you understand what I am trying to accomplish day-in and day-out for my customers?
- Can you make me look good?

Can you communicate your skills and experiences to your customer? Do you know what your customer wants? Can you convince him that you have what he wants? Employers hire people with proven skills, so tell the customer what you know. Be absolutely clear and concise, and tell the customer only what will be of value to him. Don't put it on your résumé unless you are demonstrating *industry related* achievements or that you improved productivity, increased sales, managed other people, or you have an experience that you know to be of particular interest to your targeted market.

▸ **Strategy 4:** Transmit only what your customer wants to receive (hear or see).

COMPLEXITIES OF DECISION

The employer is your ultimate customer. Let's take a closer look at him.

Interviewing and hiring decisions are never a simple matter. There are many complexities and issues pushing and pulling at the decision maker. For the purposes of our discussion, I have divided these issues into two categories: objective and subjective.

The Employer's View—Objective

The employer's view is very important. It is the objective part of the decision-making process. The employer is concerned about his business. He wants to hire the person who is best qualified for the position in terms of experience, education, and productivity. He makes sure that there is a description of all the positions that are open. These job descriptions give information about the skills required, the duties and responsibilities of the job, and the minimum experience and educational background that will be accepted. The personnel recruiter has copies of these, and if he has done his homework, he has interviewed key internal staff to further clarify what the position is and how it fits into the goals of the immediate supervisor, the department, and the organization. This does not appear to be a difficult task, but certain complexities do enter into it. For example, the recruiter's view of what the employer wants may be different from what the employer actually does want. The questions that must be asked can have two different versions:

Factual	Judgmental
What is the job the employer wants done and what are the criteria for evaluating the applicants?	What is the job the recruiter believes the employer wants done and what are the criteria for evaluating applicants?
What are the risks of a bad hire for the organization?	What does the screener believe are the risks of a bad hire for the organization?
How does this candidate compare to the others being considered?	How does the screener believe this candidate compares to the others being considered?
What is the time pressure for making the decision to hire?	What is the perceived time pressure for making the decision to hire?

It is easy to see how the subjectivity of the recruiter can impinge on the employer's objectivity, and thus on the hiring process. Why does this happen? Let's take a look.

The Decision Maker's View—Subjective

Just as we all carry our emotional baggage around with us and unconsciously allow it to affect our decisions, the decision maker (résumé reader, interviewer, recruiter) always brings his or her own personal prejudices, emotions, and knowledge to the decision-making process. He carries them with him as he confronts your résumé.

First, he reads the actual information about you that was obtained from your résumé. This knowledge is never complete. It only contains what you wrote, and is only as effective as your ability to communicate.

The disclosures you have made are, by necessity, limited in scope. A résumé is, after all, only a brief summary of the professional you. This is all it is expected to be. But with this condensed information, the decision maker must evaluate you and decide whether or not you will get an interview.

Next, his personal values and opinions enter into his thoughts, although he is probably unaware that this is happening. These biases can be as ridiculous as the fact that you are over 40 (this one is illegal, but can nevertheless be real), to the coincidence that your *alma mater* is the same college as the one his son flunked out of as a freshman. Perhaps he automatically hates you because your name is the same as that of his ex-wife. Or he could decide to interview you because you went to school in his home town. Get the picture?

It sounds as though getting the interview is a matter of getting your résumé in front of the right person, at the right time, and with enough luck to hit on his soft spots instead of his sore spots. There is actually more to it than that. A more sophisticated decision maker will ask himself questions like these:

- Will this individual get me in trouble?
- Is my job on the line?
- Will this candidate outshine me?
- Will this candidate be a good hire and therefore make me look like a hero?
- Will this candidate enhance my career?
- Am I sure that this candidate is the best hire for this position, or are there better candidates to be found?

Whether at the conscious or subconscious level, the screener's decision is affected by the answers to such questions.

Looking for a "Personality Match"

The way the résumé reader feels at a given moment can also have a direct effect on you. Has she just had a fight with her spouse? Has there been a personal disappointment in his career? Was her son just arrested for driving under the influence of alcohol? Does he think you annoy him too much with your telephone queries? Did you openly argue with her basic personal convictions? Is he responding to you at the gut level?

The personality match between you and the decision maker is not to be overlooked. Your personal style and how well it complements that of the recruiter certainly affects your fate. One new hire was told, after a succession of interviews with a major Eastern bank, "Yes, you look like you work here." He was hired to do a job for which he had no actual experience, even though the job specifications definitely required it.

Every recruiter brings her own concept of reality to the decision-making process. No two decision makers come to a decision in the same way. They will look at things differently even when their background, credentials, or level of experience and education are all the same. The way a person thinks is that person's reality.

There is an old adage that says we should never judge a man until we have walked a mile in his shoes. The wisdom of this is evident when we think of the times we have stood in judgment of someone, only to later feel sheepish when we find out why they behaved or reacted in a certain way. This can be applied to the job-seeking situation. The recruiter will judge you without being fully aware of the basis on which he is doing so. By the time he figures out that his decision was based on personal prejudices, if he ever does, it will be too late. Someone else will already have been hired.

Your job is to take as much control of these perceptions and personal truths as possible. It doesn't really matter how perfectly matched you are to the position, even if you are the *best* candidate for the job. If the person making the decision does not perceive it or believe it, you haven't got a chance.

THE COMPETITIVE EDGE

When you can approach the development of your résumé from a strategic perspective, the competitive advantage is no longer an elusive goal. To help you anticipate what the employer is looking for, I have developed two new tools: The first is the *Cross Over Strategy*, which will be discussed in this chapter. The second is an interpretive collection of recommendations from your "customers." It is the result of the newest research on what employers really want (see Chapter 4), and is for your exclusive review and examination.

THE CROSS OVER STRATEGY

The Cross Over (the Desk) Strategy will help you to develop your résumé and to be successful in your subsequent interviews. If you neglect this portion of the task, you could misfire on every major segment of the job search. Here is where the successful job seeker raises himself above the ordinary.

What Is the Cross Over Strategy?

What do prospective employers want? You should be addressing their objectives as you write your résumé. The Cross Over Strategy helps you identify specifically what the employer is looking for, particularly as their needs and objectives relate to your background and goals.

In using the Cross Over Strategy, you will benefit by learning how to better sell yourself in the interview, as well as in your résumé, and by learning how to add your perceptions of the job requirements to your résumé.

How to Do the Cross Over

The Cross Over first involves an attitude adjustment. Instead of thinking about what you want, you will think about what the employer wants. You will Cross Over the desk and put yourself in his shoes. You will try to understand his way of thinking. As you begin to plan your résumé, you are the employer.

You will need two documents to complete this strategy:

1. The Goals Definition Worksheet (p. 16)—This worksheet was completed in Chapter 2, the goals section. It defines your position objective.

   If you identified two or three different objectives, you will need to do the Cross Over Worksheet for each to determine whether one, two, or three different résumés are required.
2. The Cross Over Worksheet—Completing the worksheet on p. 32 will help you to understand your employer's needs.

   Most of us already have enough information to complete this form. If you do not, use your resources to get more information about similar companies and positions. One resource is the people you know who are knowledgeable about what is specifically needed to secure the position you want. Another resource is your local library or bookstore, in which you can find a wealth of information on various companies in the reference department. You can also write directly to the public relations departments of the companies you are interested in working for. They will be happy to send you information about their companies. Find out all you can about your prospective employer.

List the 6 to 10 experiences in your background that will be imperative "must haves" in the eyes of the employer in the left column on the Cross Over Worksheet on page 32. These are the credentials and experiences that the résumé decision-maker considers important. This is his call entirely. The following examples give a broad range of industries and titles and should prove helpful to you in developing your own *Cross Over Strategy*.

Your Objectives and Theirs

Use "Your Objective" and "Theirs" (see p. 36) to develop and refine your résumé. This is easy to complete. All you need to do is transfer the information from your Goals Definition Worksheet and from

CROSS OVER WORKSHEET

For Position Objective ______________________________

Title or Description

I. What Most Employers (Probably) Want	II. Rank Order Employers' Probable Preferences	III. List Preferences in Descending Order from Column II on this Worksheet*

*Given your objective, this is the priority ranking of what most employers probably want. Remember to put your accomplishments and preferences aside for now. This is the employer's call.

CROSS OVER WORKSHEET

For Position Objective *Chief Financial Officer*
Title or Description

I. What Most Employers (Probably) Want	II. Rank Order Employers' Probable Preferences	III. List Preferences in Descending Order from Column II on this Worksheet*
MIS	6	1. *Management Experience*
Controllership	2	2. *Controllership*
Financial Planning	3	3. *Financial Planning*
Credit	9	4. *Treasury*
Audit	7	5. *Tax*
Treasury	4	6. MIS
Tax	5	7. *Audit*
Investor Relations	8	8. *Investor Relations*
Management Experience	1	9. *Credit*

*Given your objective, this is the priority ranking of what most employers probably want. Remember to put your accomplishments and preferences aside for now. This is the employer's call.

CROSS OVER WORKSHEET

For Position Objective *Director of Communications*
Title or Description

I. What Most Employers (Probably) Want	II. Rank Order Employers' Probable Preferences	III. List Preferences in Descending Order from Column II on this Worksheet*
Electronics Industry Experience	*6*	1. *Management*
Public Relations	*5*	2. *Media Relations*
Advertising	*9*	3. *Events Planning*
Marketing	*4*	4. *Marketing*
Events Planning	*3*	5. *Public Relations*
Management	*1*	6. *Electronics Industry Experience*
New Products Promotion	*7*	7. *New Products Promotion*
Media Relations	*2*	8. *Writing*
Writing	*8*	9. *Advertising*
Government Relations	*10*	10. *Government Relations*

*Given your objective, this is the priority ranking of what most employers probably want. Remember to put your accomplishments and preferences aside for now. This is the employer's call.

CROSS OVER WORKSHEET

For Position Objective *Vice President Human Resources*
Title or Description

I. What Most Employers (Probably) Want	II. Rank Order Employers' Probable Preferences	III. List Preferences in Descending Order from Column II on this Worksheet*
Recruiting	*10*	*1. Management Experience*
Benefits	*4*	*2. Manpower Planning*
Compensation	*4*	*3. Succession Planning*
Training	*9*	*4. Compensation/Benefits*
Organizational Development	*6*	*5. Labor/Employee Relations*
Manpower Planning	*2*	*6. Organizational Development*
Succession Planning	*3*	*7. Personnel Systems*
Management Experience	*1*	*8. Career Development*
Career Development	*8*	*9. Training*
Personnel Systems	*7*	*10. Recruiting*
Labor Relations	*5*	
Employee Relations	*5*	

*Given your objective, this is the priority ranking of what most employers probably want. Remember to put your accomplishments and preferences aside for now. This is the employer's call.

column 3 of your Cross Over Worksheet. Then keep these two sets of objectives on your desk as you plan each word, every phrase, and the total format and organization of your résumé (and your entire job-search campaign, as well).

Your Objective	Their Objective
Title: *Vice President*	1. *Management Experience*
Field/Industry: *Consumer Foods*	2. *Manpower Planning*
Function: *Human Resources*	3. *Succession Planning*
Company Size: *Two billion (the larger, the better)*	4. *Compensation/Benefits*
Responsibilities: *Direct all Human Resource activities for corporation. Report to CEO. Have impact in strategic planning.*	5. *Labor/Employee Relations*
Managing Requirements: *Staff of four to eight*	6. *Organization Development*
Growth Potential: *To Senior V.P. Human Resources or move into Administration*	7. *Personnel Systems*
Environment: *Proactive; human resource oriented; close proximity to CEO*	8. *Career Development*
Salary: *$135,000 plus bonus*	9. *Training*
Location: *Northeastern United States*	10. *Recruiting*

Strategy 5 below is the one that puts you in control!

▸ **Strategy 5:** Continually cross over the desk and step into the shoes of your potential employer.

Witness the following executive jobseeker. Before the *Cross Over Strategy*, he was just running in the race. After he learned how to use this tool, he was able to let his prospective market know he understood their problems. Now the background in his résumé demonstrated he had the particular experience and skills to do the job.

> Jerry Johnson came back to the United States after seven years as a division General Manager for a Fortune 500 consumer electronics firm in Europe. The company was phasing down and opportunities were limited to none in the domestic units. Jerry elected to take his generous severance package and search for a new job. He refused outplacement assistance initially and for six months he conducted his own job search. I met Jerry after he had gone back to his company in frustration and requested outplacement. We began by analyzing his campaign. What did he do right? What did he do wrong? He had worked rather hard (nearly everyday) on his job search. The results were some interviews, but no job offer. His network was trying to help. His résumé was good. However, after careful evaluation of his objective and the résumé content, it was clear he had no sense of the changes and requirements of his target job market. In his seven year absence, the domestic consumer electronics market had changed radically. He knew that sales in his company had dropped substantially, but he had no sense of the nuances in the present marketplace.
>
> I coached him to start over. He put his résumé aside and went out to his network. He used the online business research and visited the business reference library and the association resources in his field to help him find out what the job market needed and wanted. He was resistant at first because he felt that senior people at his level should not have to ask for help. Using this new research he developed a *Cross Over Strategy* that told him how to rewrite his résumé and refocus his job search. In three months he had a new position (the one he wanted) with a smaller competitor as President.

The Cross Over gives you the power to better control the direction and overall success of your résumé. It allows you to make an educated guess about what the employer is looking for. The Cross Over Strategy gives you the competitive edge. Use it often to double check what you say and do in the résumé and in the interview.

4

The Newest Research on What Employers Really Want

How many times it thundered before Franklin took the hint! How many apples fell on Newton's head before he took the hint! Nature is always hinting at us. It hints over and over again. And suddenly, we take the hint.

Robert Frost

ABOUT THE SURVEY

Your résumé will be successful in the job market because you will be aware of what that market is saying and doing.

I conducted a survey of those who read and screen executives' résumés. What do they say? What do they want? The results of this survey* gave me the answers to these and other questions.

In the past several years, there has been an explosion of outplacement firms and career counselors who coach and counsel more job seekers than ever before. There are now more "coached" résumés in the job market, and these are competing with yours. How are the résumé readers responding to "professionally coached" résumés?

The market target for executives includes such people as CEOs, other senior officers, corporate recruiters, executive recruiters, and personnel managers. Individuals from these fields were selected for this research study on the assumption that they are the ones who make decisions about the future of each executive résumé that crosses their desk. There was a high response rate of 34 percent from this cross-section of decision makers and organizations. Comments were received that verify the importance of the subject. The remark below was reflected in many of the unsolicited notes and phone calls:

> Glad to be asked . . . important subject . . . no one has ever asked me how or what I want.
>
> Nicholas Podoba
> Corporate Director Human Resources
> International Minerals & Chemicals

* For more details on how the survey was conducted, see the Appendix.

The key topic responses fall into six major areas:

- Three revelations
- Biggest turn-ons
- Biggest turn-offs
- Résumé structure
- Credentials
- Reaction to out-of-the-ordinary experiences
- Other relevant information

Read through this chapter quickly the first time. Then go back to each section as you need it during the development phase of your résumé.

The large volume and range of responses to this survey show that, even though there is an abundance of career counseling, outplacement services, and self-help books and articles, employers are aware that there is too much ambiguity about what is wanted and what is appropriate today. This research should prove extremely helpful because it clears up the jobseekers uncertainty with hard data on what employers really want.

THREE REVELATIONS

The survey revealed three big surprises that should cause you to rethink the strategic approach to your particular job market. These findings could be the reason why some highly qualified people are not getting their résumés through the initial reading and into the "to be interviewed" file.

The three revelations are:

1. Senior executives usually don't screen executive résumés.
2. Interviews can be granted without inspecting résumés.
3. A letter alone is not likely to land an interview.

Initial Résumé Readers

A rule for years has been: Send your résumé to a senior official as high in the organization as possible. Executives, in particular, are told to aim their résumés only at the top.

The most surprising revelation was that senior executives (chief executive officer, chief operating officer, president, managing partner, executive or senior vice president) rarely take the time to review unsolicited résumés themselves.

The survey results show that *initial* résumé screening is done by those at the managerial level (38 percent) and those at the directorial level (31 percent), and that the job titles of these managers and directors indicate that the overwhelming majority are in personnel or human resource departments.

Although 33 percent of those surveyed said they recruit at salaries of up to $50,000, these people are also making decisions about higher-level candidates.

What Does This Mean to You?

This research reveals several things that are important to the executive seeking a high-level position:

1. The first "weeding out" process is usually done at the lower levels in the organization.
2. The high-level executive candidates must prepare their résumés to elicit positive initial responses at lower levels in the organization (not just from the highest ranking officials).
3. If reaching the top of the organization is your target, then weapons other than the résumé should be used to break down the door.

Interviews Without First Seeing Résumés

Another startling find was that 55 percent of all survey respondents said that they would grant an interview without first seeing some form of documentation (résumé, letter, biography, etc.). A minority said they would not.

It has long been thought that the executive job candidate must send a résumé before she would be granted an interview. Although this is still true with many companies, it is no longer the case in many instances. There is another way to get the interview.

What Does This Mean to You?

If you don't need to have a résumé precede you, what do you need? A personal, reliable referral. Look at some of the comments made by survey respondents about the conditions under which they would be willing to interview a job seeker without first reviewing a résumé:

> If the individual was referred to me on a personal basis and the applicant had great credentials.
>
> Vice President, Human Resources
Insurance/Financial Services Firm

> Only if the chief executive/board of directors members or personal friends request it and timing is a factor.
>
> Robert Pdgorski
Director of Employment
Northrop Corporation
Rolling Meadows

> If referred by someone in whom I have extreme confidence and whose judgment I can trust.
>
> Vice President, Human Resources
Bank & Trust Company
Houston

Survey statistics indicate that executive recruiters may be more receptive than their corporate counterparts, but only if the circumstances are right. These are some of the written comments from executive search firms regarding granting interviews without résumés.

> If the person is aggressive or creative enough to get me to do it, then he or she is probably worth seeing.
>
> Charles Jett
> McFeeley, Wackerle, & Jett
> Chicago

> If a phone interview is successful and I am in a hurry to present a candidate.
>
> Consultant
> Executive Recruiting Firm
> Los Angeles

> . . . will base judgment on an in-depth phone conversation in lieu of a résumé.
>
> Susan A. Jaeger
> S. A. Jaeger & Company, Inc.
> Oak Brook

Does this mean you should try to get a face-to-face meeting for yourself? It is worth a try.

Use all the resources available to you to get this meeting. The above statistics and statements show that prospective employers are more amenable than you might think. Of course, an excellent referral is always helpful; the personal referral is the way in. Executive recruiters still need to be persuaded. Their comments say "convince me." The referral will help to persuade and convince.

An outplacement consultant, who has advised hundreds of out-of-work executives on obtaining interviews, concurs:

> You are probably better off if you can get in without even showing a résumé.
>
> Brad W. Harper
> Principal
> Nelson-Harper & Associates
> Phoenix Outplacement Firm

Why are you better off getting in without a résumé? Because you will have more control over that important first impression. You won't be judged merely on the basis of a piece of paper, without ever having been seen or spoken to in person. However, if you can't get in without a résumé, then use this book to help you prepare the best one possible. In any event, you will need one eventually. Whether yours will be seen before, during, or after the interview remains open.

▸ **Strategy 6:** Use your résumé as little as possible—only when you must!

LETTERS ALONE WON'T DO THE JOB

Although a majority of survey participants said they would grant an interview without first seeing some documentation, a letter alone is not the way to get the interview appointment. More than two-thirds (68 percent) said "no" when asked, "Will you respond favorably to a letter (rather than a résumé)?" Only 32 percent said "yes." The executive recruiters are only slightly more open to a letter than are the total survey population shown above. Approximately 60 percent voted "no" and 40 percent said "yes."

The following comments show how the decision makers decide whether to grant an interview to someone who has sent only a letter:

> Not necessarily. I'll respond to creative marketing as long as it helps me understand what they can do . . . especially if they have the initiative to personally call . . . most direct mail gets trashed.
>
> Paul Sniffin
> New Options Group, Inc.
> Baltimore Outplacement Firm

> Never—only letter with résumé.
>
> Tony Ferracane
> Personnel Director
> Ingalls Memorial Hospital
> Harvey

Depends. If letter respondent looks perfect, will respond; otherwise discard.

Chief Financial Officer
National Transportation Carrier
Chicago

What Does This Mean to You?

A letter, then, is not the preferred way to communicate your desire for the job. However, if you do decide to send a letter, it must be:

Strategic
Creative
Targeted
Timely

BIGGEST TURN-ONS

Fifty-one percent of the respondents voted for "neatness" as the number one turn-on. "Typesetting" received 21 percent of the votes, and "lots of white space" received 18 percent.

Neatness

You have been told that neatness counts ever since you first learned to write. When you consider that your résumé can affect the rest of your life, you can begin to understand the importance of the way it looks. If it looks inviting to read, it will be read, even if the recruiter is overworked and it's 11:00 P.M. A neat résumé says, "Look at me. I'm easy to read. I won't take much of your time."

Neatness projects a subtle message that makes your résumé stand out. Just as a busy editor won't read a messy, illegible manuscript, neither will a busy recruiter read a résumé that is not neat and clear. Even if you use a personal computer, there are still rules to follow. Use the same rules that writers must follow when submitting a manuscript. For example, never use erasable bond paper, because it smudges. Use, instead, high-quality paper with a high rag content. Also, use a letter-quality printer, such as a daisy wheel or laser. Never use a dot-matrix printer, because it produces copy that is hard on the eyes. Finally, make sure that your résumé looks neat at first glance. Are there misspelled words? Have you used a lot of White Out®, or crossed out words? Fix it!

Typesetting

As many as 21 percent voted for typesetting as a turn-on. Does this new data mean that typesetting is welcomed, and for some screeners, actually preferred?

I have always advised job hunters to avoid typesetting because I believe it tells the reader there is a grand campaign in motion. Who would bother to typeset for one or two résumés? Nonetheless, this data suggests it is now acceptable to typeset.

This preference for typesetting may be a response to the widespread use of computers with laser technology that allows for crisp and bold typeface. Perhaps this new technology can look like typesetting to the hurried reader's eye. Unless you are in a field that relies heavily on promotion, such as public relations or advertising, I still recommend a typewritten format.

Lots of White Space

Those who rated "white space" highly are saying, "Make your résumé easy to read." Another reason it is rated highly is because résumé readers like to write notes in the margins. Make the margins generous on all four sides.

Other turn-ons mentioned were:

- Good organization
- Accuracy
- Brevity
- Focus

Good Organization

Recruiters and other résumé readers are saying over and over, "the easier you can make my résumé reading, the more likely I'll consider your résumé favorably."

How can you make their reading easier? Let's find out by looking at their comments:

- Good outline format to scan for highlights.
- Organized layout is very important.
- Logical presentation.

No one has the time to wade through your résumé to find the relevant information. Each separate section should be easy to find. The recruiter wants to be able to scan your résumé quickly so that he can relate it to a job now open or future positions that may develop.

Readers are also drawing inferences about you from what they see in your résumé. They may think, "If this is the way you organize your résumé, maybe this is the way you would organize your work life."

Accuracy

Recruiters for corporations and executive search firms can easily spot exaggeration and embellishment. They frown upon both of these. Typical infringements of these are claiming to have achieved something singlehandedly when it is obviously a team achievement or claiming an unprovable (e.g. 80% or some such) increase in productivity or profit.

Their comments say to be brief, accurate, honest, and simple. Be factual: tell what you did and what the result was. For example, consider these two statements that an accounting executive might use:

1. Responsible for collections from delinquent accounts.
2. Developed and wrote new procedures for collections from delinquent accounts that saved 14 staff hours per week and reduced days sales outstanding 28 percent.

The second statement is not only factual, but also shows results by revealing the impact the work had on the accounting department. In addition, the number 14 is more believable than using a percentage. Use numbers whenever possible rather than the overused percentages that are now filling up the "coached" résumés.

Don't say that you are "smart," "successful," and have a "track record." Demonstrate it in your résumé through factual examples.

Brevity

Respondents said they want résumés that are short and sweet, precise, succinct and to the point.

They want a brief résumé in which the executive has taken the time and effort to condense a long and awkward paragraph into one or two clear, concise sentences. Concise says to the reader, "I understand your time constraints and respect them."

Some years ago, I worked with an academic client who brought me a 15-page résumé to review. To the other extreme, one executive search consultant I know received a résumé that he has not been able to forget—a letter that only said, "Have car; own home. Let's talk." (Incidentally, he remembers that résumé, but he quickly and intentionally forgot the person who sent it.)

You should be concise, but obviously not ridiculous. A résumé of one or two pages should be sufficient.

Focus

To show exactly what you can do, your résumé should concentrate on only one job objective. For many experienced people, the job search takes longer than it should because their résumés reveal all of the work experiences they have ever had. One would almost think that they can do anything—or that they are "Jacks of all trades and masters of none!"

Survey responses show that résumé readers are only interested in quickly finding out what it is you can do for their organizations and why you are qualified to do it.

If you have worked in more than two different fields, such as general management, sales management, and finance, and want to simultaneously look for a position in all of these fields, you will probably need more than one résumé. Focus each one. Don't try to save time by developing only one résumé to accomplish all three objectives. You will only hurt your chances for success. Companies want to know that you excel in one or two specialties, not that you've had a few years experience in each of several fields.

Résumé readers become burdened when more than a quick overview of your résumé is required. It is not that these screeners are lazy; it is a matter of time and energy. Deciding who you are and where you belong in their company is your job, not theirs.

BIGGEST TURN-OFFS

Two items almost tied for first place as the number one turn-off. "Lengthiness" was cited by 26 percent of the respondents, and "typos, misspellings, poor grammar" were identified by 25 percent. Next was "sloppiness," mentioned by 15 percent, followed by a three-way tie with "photographs" and "exaggerations" at 11 percent each and "clutter" (little white space and narrow margins) at 10 percent.

Lengthiness

A résumé that runs longer than two pages, even if it is the résumé of a high-level senior executive, shows disrespect for the reader. Longer résumés take too much time to read and are generally boring. Another problem is that they are often confusing; it is too hard for the reader to figure out how his organization can use the candidate.

Be assured that if your résumé runs longer than two pages, it can be shortened without leaving out any essential information. I have had clients who started with as many as 17 to 25 pages of career accomplishments, but who were able to reduce that down to a two-page résumé.

There are those recruiters whose preference is closer to one page; more than two pages is a tremendous turn-off. Not only is it time consuming, but it may also give the impression that the candidate, who appears to be at the senior level, is actually consumed by detail and is not a strategic thinker.

Three survey participants expressed this turn-off as follows:

- "Excessive length"
- "Too long or not factual"
- "More than 2 pages"

Typos, Misspellings, Grammar

Most computer wordprocessing programs have spelling-check functions and internal dictionaries; and proofreaders are easy to find. It is inexcusable that a typo would show up on anyone's résumé or correspondence. Yet, survey respondents declare that typos are found much too frequently.

A typo makes the reader suspect that the writer may have poor work habits, may not be dependable, is careless, or simply does not care enough to follow through and proofread his own work.

Misspellings, particularly of the names of people you are trying to influence, are always an affront. A phone call to a secretary will give you the opportunity to check that "Smyth" is not "Smith."

This respondent, an executive recruiter, should not have to say that the biggest turn-off in the résumés he reviews is:

> Spelling or grammatical errors.
>
> John S. Rothchild
> Director, Human Resources
> Grant Thornton
> Chicago

Sloppiness

Recruiters say that they actually receive résumés with coffee stains, smudges, wrinkles, and correction fluid. There is no excuse for this on your reports and correspondence on the job, let alone a professional résumé! Recruiters also dislike typeovers, poor-quality photocopies, and, again, résumés typed on erasable bond paper. A sloppy résumé is hard to read and may even cause eyestrain. It also tells the decision maker that the person who sent it does not care about the quality of his work.

Photographs

A photograph on a résumé is a clear signal that the candidate is egotistical as well as behind the times. Not only does the photograph distract the reader's attention away from the résumé, but it also distorts his view. Don't give him the opportunity to discard your résumé because your photo reminds him of an unreasonable boss who once cost him a promotion. Furthermore, a photo can give a false impression. Many people unconsciously place certain attributes with certain facial features. For example, there are those who falsely associate a weak chin with a weak intellect. Your photo might be a great asset, but don't take the chance. Let the recruiter see you for the first time in person so that your appearance, your personality, and your mind can all work together for your greatest benefit.

Until the early 1960s, before the Civil Rights Act of 1964 made it illegal for employers to discriminate against job candidates, photos were acceptable. Photographs make recruiters susceptible to possible charges of discrimination in hiring practices. Rather than take a chance, some recruiters refuse to interview anyone who sends in a résumé displaying a photo.

This turn-off provoked one survey participant to express his displeasure at a résumé with a photograph that stated

> Picture of individual—current employer's name withheld.
>
> Norman E. Van Maldegiam
> Principal
> Van Maldegiam Associates
> Chicago

Exaggerations

Exaggeration is obvious to the experienced résumé reader. It will be spotted immediately. Exaggerations imply that the person is not honest; is unsure of his capabilities, strengths, and skills; or has nothing substantial to offer. One respondent summed it up:

> Falsified information or misleading and exaggerated claims are a turn-off.
>
> Corporate Director of Personnel
> A Midwest Financial Institution
> Indianapolis

Clutter

A résumé with too many words and little white space is uninviting, unattractive, and distracting. It makes the reader's job harder. A survey respondent indicated clutter as a turn-off because it hinders reading:

> Inability to quickly find the basic details (career history and personal data).
>
> Toni Smith
> Vice President
> Spencer Stuart
> Chicago

SURVEY RESULTS ON RÉSUMÉ STRUCTURE

Functional Résumés

The survey asked résumé readers, "Will you respond favorably to a functional résumé (a résumé that does not have the typical list of employers in chronological order)? If yes, tell why or when."

For many job seekers, this is a critical question. A chronological résumé is not always appropriate because it tells too much or tells things that shouldn't be told. This new data finds that 54 percent of those queried would *not* respond favorably to a purely functional résumé. Interestingly, 46 percent said they would respond favorably.

"No" to Functional Résumés

Those employers who said "no" to functional résumés gave reasons similar to these respondents:

> . . . functional résumés are red flags to me indicating someone who has changed jobs too often, has gaps in history, thinks they are too old, or has had little career direction.
>
> Corporate Recruiter
Consumer Foods Company
Glenview
>
> Dislike functionals . . . functionals bury the facts.
>
> Donald Mershon
Vice President
Lutron
Coopersberg
>
> Not particularly . . . too difficult to decipher and wonder what is being "hidden."
>
> Sara Snoy
Vice President Personnel
Alexander & Alexander, Inc.
Chicago

"Yes" to Functional Résumés

Those who said "yes" to functional résumés explained their thinking as follows:

> Yes, if done well. . . . can tell more in less space.
>
> Robert I. Mulford
President
Mulford Moreland & Associates
San Jose Area Outplacement Firm

Yes, occasionally—if hard-to-fill requirement and functional résumé well-developed.

Personnel Representative
High Tech Electronics Corporation
Los Angeles

At first, yes. However, I will not grant a personal interview on a functional outline/broadcast letter.

Director Employment & Staffing
Mid-Size Healthcare Provider
Stamford

Only if chronological dates are outlined at bottom.

Employment Manager
International Bank
Washington, DC

Yes, if tied to where they did it. However, some of these become difficult to follow and may be cover-ups.

Joyce L. Watts
Formerly Assistant Dean,
Career Placement
J.L. Kellogg Graduate School
of Management
Northwestern University
Evanston

Yes, first question is "What has this person done/achieved and is background applicable to search?" If functional gets this done—fine.

Thomas Nossem
Vice President Human Resources
Leo Burnett
Chicago

What Does This Mean to You?

If you do decide to use a functional format, the preciseness of its focus must be clear to the reader. Sometimes, the functional is the only choice you have. However, put in the necessary effort to make it work for you (more about this in Chapter 6).

Maximum Length of Résumé

The largest vote (79 percent) was for a maximum length of two pages. Approximately 10 percent prefer one page and, surprisingly, another 10 percent like three or more pages. A minority of 1 percent said it doesn't matter.

The best advice is to pay close attention to length. Perhaps it can be summed up best by quoting Mies Van der Rohe, the renowned Chicago architect, who said, "Less is more." These statements from survey participants tend to agree with him. Respondents wrote:

> One page preferred . . . for senior management, 2 to 3 pages OK.
>
> Manager Human Resources
> Fortune 500 Manufacturing Firm
> Dayton

> One page ideal . . . two pages only for 20 years experience.
>
> Director Organizational Planning
> & Placement
> Leading Retail Organization
> Chicago

> I've seen many [résumés] 4 pages long and some much longer (one was 8 pages long). An executive should be able to summarize his/her background. More than 2 pages is usually sent by folks with ego problems—I've seen several signed by "Mr. So & So" that listed accomplishments and memberships that are not relevant.
>
> Natalie Kelly
> Manager Personnel Services
> Canteen Corporation
> Chicago

What Does This Mean to You?

A maximum of two pages is the safest rule. A two-page résumé is almost never wrong, while a one-page résumé only works well for the junior level applicant because of his or her shorter career history.

Color Preference of Paper

Twenty-one percent of those responding prefer white paper while 31 percent want cream/buff. Forty-four percent had no preference. Only 2 percent preferred grey paper.

> Some people believe that résumés on colored paper stand out, so they will be called for an interview. They are only fooling themselves. What matters is the content.
>
> Sharon Gadberry, Ph.D.
> President
> Transitions Management Group
> San Francisco-Based Outplacement Firm

Historically, the best advice from many résumé experts has been to choose white paper. The rationale behind this advice still has some value. Colored paper and typesetting could imply that the candidate was professionally coached and anxious to get a new job. After all, who would invest in colored paper and typesetting for only one or two résumés?

Although Gadberry's advice is excellent when strategizing and refining the subtleties of the job hunt, the new research says that the cream/buff color is not only acceptable, but actually preferred by nearly one-third of the respondents.

What Does This Mean to You?

Consider these four points:

- Content is of primary importance and using color to get attention is inappropriate.
- Decision makers like cream/buff and white. They don't seem to care for grey.
- The 44 percent who say they do not have a color preference could also be saying they simply do not have *strong* feelings about paper color.

- It is recommended to stay with white or cream/buff and concentrate more on content.

Placement of Educational Data

Fifty percent of those surveyed say the end of the résumé is the best place to insert your educational background. Another 29 percent prefer the top of the first page. The remaining 21 percent expressed no preference.

It is not as clear where to place this information when analyzing the executive recruiter responses. Approximately 40 percent prefer the top of the first page, while another 40 percent said it does not matter. The remaining 20 percent prefer the end. Look at some of the comments regarding placement of this material:

Place at the end:

End . . . work experience more relevant to executive level.

Robert K. Wilmouth
President and CEO
National Futures Association
Chicago

End . . . A candidate for an executive position had better have something more relevant to offer than a degree from 5, 10, or 15 years ago.

Sara Snoy
Vice President Personnel
Alexander and Alexander, Inc.
Chicago

End . . . it is history; where a person goes to school is not that important.

First Vice President
Major Midwestern Bank
Chicago

Place at the beginning or top:

Top of first page . . . want to know they meet educational requirements.

Herbert B. Gofman
Vice President
Bankers Trust Company
New York

Top, because it sets the stage for the person's experience.

James A. Faletti
Director of Human Resources
MCI Corporation
Chicago

Alternatively:

Top . . . for recent graduates. End . . . for experienced people.

Margaret F. Higgins
Vice President Employee Relations
Citicorp Savings
Singapore

Top, if impressive; end, if not.

Lionel Sidlin
Division Manager Human Resources
Eaton Corporation
Carol Stream

Top for scientific/technical . . . key screening; . . . end for experienced.

Susan Crowe
Personnel Director
Abbott Laboratories
North Chicago

Let the candidate decide; it's an indication of what they're selling.

Stephen C. Ford
President
Fitzgerald, Stevens, Ford, Inc.
Boston-Based Outplacement Firm

Don't care as long as it's there.

Toby Antrim
Manager, Headquarters Recruiting
Connecticut National Bank
Hartford

No preference.

Ronald Cate
Senior Director Human Resources
Ameritech Services, Inc
Chicago

What Does This Mean to You?

In general, experience is more important and should appear before educational data. At this point in your career if you're an executive or have 10 or more years of experience, accomplishments on the job are more important than education. You must decide for yourself where to place your educational data; however, if these two criteria apply to you, you may decide to place your education at the top:

1. If you graduated from a top level school or have exceedingly impressive educational credentials.
2. If your degree is specifically connected to your objective. For example, a degree in accounting is viable for a position as a controller or an accountant; a technical degree is pertinent if you are seeking a position in the technical field or with a high-tech company.

If your college or university major doesn't match the job you want, keep this information at the end of the résumé. You may not even want to disclose your major on your résumé.

SURVEY RESULTS ON CREDENTIALS

How important is a graduate degree, especially the M.B.A.? This is one credential that some of my senior outplacement clients lack.

They feel that this may hurt them in the initial screening of their résumés. This view is typical and pervasive among executive job seekers. To compare this view to reality in the executive marketplace, the survey asked résumé readers, "How important is a graduate degree? Why?" Their responses are indicated below.

Graduate Degree

More than half (56 percent) said they think a graduate degree is very important. Less than one-third (29 percent) think it is not very important. The remaining 14 percent said it depends on the position. A total of 60 percent of the executive recruiters prefer a graduate degree, while 30 percent say it should be job related and 10 percent see it as not very important.

Consider these respondents' comments on the importance of a graduate degree:

> Quite important, if right degree.
>
> Robert A Schmitz
> President and CEO
> Richard D. Irwin
> Division of Times-Mirror
> Homewood

> Important. We like to hire M.B.A.s.
>
> Anthony Spier
> President
> International Division
> AM International
> Rolling Meadows

> For certain positions, it is required. However, too high a degree or multiple degrees may be a drawback.
>
> F. Craig Barber
> President
> F. Craig Barber Outplacement Counseling
> Minneapolis

It all depends . . . at best, it shows a motivation, and also the ability to handle advanced work.

Sherman Rosen
Vice President Human Resources
Hartmarx Corporation
Chicago

I don't think it is that important . . . only for certain highly specialized positions (e.g., an internal consultant with a master's degree has more sophisticated analytical skills); however, not necessary for line positions.

William Huck
Formerly Vice President Human Resources
American National Bank
Chicago

The more mature the candidate and the stronger the accomplishments, the less important a graduate degree (or other degree) becomes.

Michael Murphy
President
The Signet Group
Chicago

Not very important. It's what you have done that counts.

Don Mershon
Vice President
Lutron
Coopersburg

Not very important. Experience remains the best teacher.

Judith Harper
Manager Human Resources
McCormick & Company, Inc.
Hayward

Very important . . . employer always prefers.

Principal
Executive Search Firm
Los Angeles

Depends on client specification and culture.

Vice President
Executive Recruiting Firm
Chicago

. . . becomes less important as individual gains experience.

Partner
Executive Search Firm
St. Louis

Type of Graduate Degree Preferred

Of the respondents preferring the graduate degree, the most desired, by a 52 percent majority, is the M.B.A. Although 5 percent preferred "another type" of graduate degree and 1 percent said it "depends" on the position, 41 percent claimed it just "does not matter" what kind of graduate degree the candidate has.

What Does This Mean to You?

The graduate degree preferences are quite surprising. Only a little over half think a graduate degree is important at all, and of those, only 52 percent actually prefer an M.B.A. degree. If you do have a graduate degree, particularly from a top school, display it proudly. If not, don't panic. According to those decision makers who responded to the research survey, the recruiters are primarily looking at your experience.

Undergraduate Degree

A total of 87 percent said that an undergraduate degree is "very important" for an executive candidate. Approximately 4 percent voted "not very" important and 9 percent said it depends on the position. As many as 13 percent, then, are not insistent about requiring an undergraduate degree. These are willing to at least consider the possibility that an individual could land an executive position without a bachelor's degree.

Type of Undergraduate Degree Preferred

Forty-four percent of those surveyed want business degrees and 31 percent want a degree in the technical field. Only 17 percent wanted liberal arts majors. The category called "other" was preferred by 3 percent of the respondents. A good number (more than 50 percent) of the survey participants wrote in "depends . . . upon position . . . and/or other educational experience."

The executive recruiters had an unusual spread (certainly contrary to the general total population percentages above). "Business" was the major preferred by 29 percent, "technical" by 24 percent, "liberal arts" by 27 percent, and 24 percent voted for "other." Nearly half added, "depends on position."

What Does This Mean to You?

The executive recruiter's preference is designated by the individual client company. Their preference curve is more reflective of either the current work they have in-house or of whether they are an industry or functional specialist. Since each search is driven by the client's requirements, you need to know what type of undergraduate degree is preferred for someone with your career objective. If you don't know, use your network/resources to find out. If the degree you have is not appropriate to your objective, leave your major off your résumé.

Is Experience in Industry Essential?

Not even half of those surveyed (45 percent) think industry experience is "essential." Another 23 percent say it's "nice to have" and almost a third (32 percent) believe it "does not matter."

According to the executive recruiters, 56 percent say industry experience is "essential." The remaining votes were split evenly between "nice to have" and "does not matter."

Here are some comments on the importance of previous experience in the industry:

> Related experience or direct experience helps . . . but they (candidates) must show proven track record in anything they've done.
>
> Paul Sniffen
> President
> New Options Group, Inc.
> Baltimore-Based Outplacement Firm

> Not always, but preferred.
>
> A. R. Swayne
> Vice President Human Relations
> Alberto-Culver
> Franklin Park

> It's a definite plus for senior candidates.
>
> Corporate Staff Recruiter
> Mid-Size Telecommunications Co.
> Santa Monica

> . . . very important for a technical or scientific position; otherwise it varies according to the job.
>
> John G. Nathan
> Employment Staffing Representative
> Hoffmann-LaRoche, Inc.
> Nutley

> No, but having significant experience in other industries sharing common characteristics . . . is necessary.
>
> Michael Badger, Ph.D.
> President
> Northwest Consulting Group
> Seattle-Based Outplacement Firm

Preferred Number of Previous Employers

The survey asked, "Is your preference several employers or one?" The response was split rather closely among the survey participants:

- 44 percent prefer "several"
- 40 percent prefer "one or two"
- 16 percent prefer "other"

In the executive recruiter group, having had several employers was favored:

- 62 percent prefer "several"
- 25 percent prefer "one or two"
- 13 percent say "it depends on situation"

These comments reveal the reasons for the preferences of both survey populations:

> One (or two) employers demonstrates stability.
>
> John Nathan
Employment Staffing Representative
Hoffman-LaRoche Inc.
Nutley

> Usually several . . . depends on level or amount of time with each.
>
> Russ Ringl
Vice President Human Resources
Playboy Industries
Chicago

> Someone who has only been with one company worries me.
>
> Assistant Vice President
Major Financial Institution
Milwaukee

> Experience and tenure more important than number.
>
> Nicholas Podoba
Corporate Director Human Resources
International Minerals & Chemicals
Mundelein

Too much job hopping, particularly without a clearly evident career path, is a negative.

President
Executive Search Firm
New York

Two to four, all related to core experience, gives broader experience.

Nancy Schellhous
President
Promark Company
Cincinnati-Based Outplacement Firm

What Does This Mean to You?

Two to four employers that reflect appropriate experience and a stable tenure is optimum. If your career history is too long or has too many employers, see the section on "How to Handle Problems" in Chapter 6.

Kinds of Previous Employers

The survey also asked résumé readers what kinds of previous employers they preferred candidates to have. Some respondents specified kinds of employers as: "big, major, related industries," and "for profit."

Their choices were verified by the following comments:

Three, large, well-managed companies.

Robert Swain
Chairman
Swain & Swain, Inc.
New York-Based Outplacement Firm

Prefer both large and small size firms.

Mary Ann Rafferty
Manager Human Resources
Zellerbach Paper Company
San Francisco

If not my industry—résumé should portray why experience is valuable to me.

Jack M. Bilson, Jr.
Manager Professional Employment
UNISYS Corporation
Paoli

Related industries.

Director of Management Employment
Major Telecommunications Company
Detroit

What Does This Mean to You?

In essence, if the organization(s) you have been associated with is (are) well-known for being an industry leader or an innovator in new technology, you will want to make sure your company affiliation has center-stage positioning on your résumé.

REACTION TO OUT-OF-THE-ORDINARY EXPERIENCES

To guide résumé writers in deciding whether an unusual experience should or should not be included in their résumés, the survey asked, "What is your reaction to out-of-the-ordinary experiences (e.g., trip for one year around the world; self-employed for five years or more)?"

Of the individuals surveyed, the split is almost equal:

- 30 percent "in favor"
- 31 percent "not in favor"
- 25 percent said "it does not matter"
- 14 percent said "it depends on situation"

Although the responses to this question are fairly evenly divided, the comments indicate that out-of-the-ordinary experiences are a controversial issue that needs to be handled carefully.

Reasons for unfavorable votes:

Generally negative—will always wonder if candidate will do it again.

Randall Rakow
Vice President Human Resources
Avery Corporation
Chicago

Concern if they would fit into a team environment.

William Walter
President
U. S. Division
Acco International
Wheeling

Raises questions that must be answered.

Employment Supervisor
Major Oil Company
Los Angeles

Can work against rather than for . . .

Hank Provost
Personnel Manager
Motorola, Inc.
Franklin Park

Can be a positive cover-up for a gap in employment or some other unfavorable situation.

Recruitment Manager
Major Healthcare Association
Chicago

This type of information should be left to the interview.

Jim Ridings
Vice President
Union Bank
Los Angeles

Favorable comments:

Often favorable, depending on the applicant's perception of the gain from the experience, how it is communicated, and if particularly useful disciplines have been acquired at the time.

Tom Ciesielski
Vice President
Federal Reserve Bank
Chicago

Can be a real plus, especially if self-employed. Other nonwork related experience less important.

T. Hall
Vice President &
Director Human Resources
Irwin Union Bank
Columbus

Exploration is fine. My next question is what did he/she learn from it and how can he/she apply it here?

Gary Tackett
Director Organization Development
Information Resources
Chicago

OK—sometimes gives individual breadth of experience to see the bigger picture.

Robert K. Wilmouth
President and CEO
National Futures Association
Chicago

Generally positive if it's valid and not an excuse for being unemployed.

Nancy Seever
Assistant Vice President
The First National Bank of Chicago
Chicago

What Does This Mean to You?

It is evident by the comments that this is highly confusing. Some said that out-of-the-ordinary experiences are an asset; others felt quite differently. The key issue is whether anything was accomplished that is marketable. If you do decide to include an experience that you may have had, be sure to show the reader exactly what the experience did for you and how it can benefit him.

OTHER SURVEY RESULTS

This question generated the greatest amount of comments: "In addition to education, professional and other experiences, and references, what else would you want to know about a person (via résumé) *before* you meet or interview him/her?"

There were some who did not respond, and there were a few who wrote a rendition of "nothing else." At least half listed one or more items that they would like to know. Their comments fall into seven categories:

1. Objectives and motivators
2. Qualifications and accomplishments
3. Professional and community leadership
4. Personal data
5. Communication skills; management and work style
6. Salary
7. Other relevant information

Your Objectives and Motivators

These respondents want to know what you want in a job and why; what drives you and motivates you; what job you are seeking; why you are leaving your present company; what you want to achieve in your next position; and why you are interested in seeking a new position.

Some Advice

Make sure that your résumé clearly states what you want. This information does not have to be limited to only one section. Indeed, using a written heading and the word "objective" on your résumé can limit its usage. Also, don't make statements that can be seen as a negative, such as don't see eye to eye with boss.

Your Qualifications and Accomplishments

Your potential customers are interested in specifics that detail in concise terms how you are qualified. They want to know what you have actually done on the job, what sets you apart from all the other candidates, what you see as your key strengths, how you relate these strengths to the position you seek, and how you are qualified to do the job. Your history of progressions, types of positions, capabilities, accomplishments, and results add up to who you are professionally.

Some Advice

Be creative and factual. Strategically target what you want with what your customer is looking for (see the Cross Over Strategy).

Your Professional and Community Leadership

Résumé readers are interested in outside activities that are related to your professional and personal development. These may include your professional and community affiliations, leadership roles, honors and awards, speeches, publications, and outside interests.

Some Advice

If your professional community activity demonstrates leadership, or in some way relates to either your objective or their objectives, give this information proudly.

Your Personal Data

Some of the respondents indicated that they wanted some very specific personal information, such as your age, marital status, and information about your children and your family. Though these questions go beyond legal boundaries, they are, indeed, asked. You should be prepared to give a factual answer despite the obvious legal implications.

Some Advice

The time to reveal this information is as late as possible in the interview process. Do not give this data in any written documentation. Even in the liberated 80s, such information can still be detrimental to your successful job search.

Your Communication Skills, Management, and Work Style

They want to know who you are, how well you write, what your people skills are, and what your style in management is. Your résumé will give them hints about these things and could give you that competitive edge.

Some Advice

Be careful. Pay close attention to form, style, and the selection of words. These things can distinguish you from others. One senior executive wrote in the qualifications summary, "Able to get to the heart of the matter."

Your Salary History

Anyone seeking to make a purchase, whether of services or goods, wants to know, "How much does it cost?" It is not surprising, then, that recruiters would like to know about your salary history and requirements.

Some Advice

Putting your salary history on your résumé makes it easy for the decision maker to put it in the "no" pile. If your requirements and history are higher than what this company wants to pay, your résumé may not get a second look; if your salary has been too low, it may be thought that your work is not on their level. Avoid putting this information on your résumé. Don't tell anyone but an executive recruiter (and put this data in your cover letter only). However, if an employer is emphatic about not considering you without your salary history, you may decide to give it.

OTHER RELEVANT INFORMATION

Your grade point average may be another item requested, but this does not make sense for anyone who is experienced.

One thing the résumé reader wants is an explanation for lapses of time. Be careful how you handle this. There are ways of formatting your résumé to handle these lapses. See "How to Handle Problems Unique to Your Background" in Chapter 6.

Your potential customer may have an interest in your willingness to relocate. If you have space, this is good to add. However, if you are not open to relocation, it is safer to leave it off. After all, you do want the opportunity to be interviewed.

Who you know in their company—if anyone is of interest to the résumé screener. If you believe the name of the person you know would be helpful, put this in the cover letter; never in the résumé.

Many interviewers will want references upfront: names, addresses, and telephone numbers. However, do not give references until your discussions are at the "we're serious" level.

A FINAL WORD

The decision maker's mission is a dual role. In the first screening, he or she wants to eliminate those résumés that are unsuitable so that more time can be spent to fulfill a primary goal—to find the right candidate for the company or the client. These screeners want enough information from your résumé so that they can put you in either the "no" or the "maybe" pile. Your goal is to avoid the "no" pile, and, ultimately, to be invited to a face-to-face interview. Therefore, be careful about what information you put on your résumé.

5

Get Set: Assess What You Bring to the Table

. . . (the executive) who qualifies himself well for his calling never fails of employment.

Thomas Jefferson
1826

This chapter could be subtitled:

If You Don't Know Who You Are . . .
Nobody Else Will!

A self-inventory of your assets and liabilities is critical to finding the right position. This is not just any job, but a career-growth opportunity that allows you to do what you enjoy most.

You must test, in your own mind, whether or not the people you report to, as well as those you supervise, agree with your self-assessment. This mental testing is necessary for an accurate evaluation.

The best advice is to consistently and thoroughly follow strategy 7.

▸ **Strategy 7:** Know thyself.

You will want to know the answers to the following questions:

- What are your assets?
- What are your liabilities?
- What are your skills?
- What skills do you enjoy using at work?
- What have you done?
- What has been your impact on your employer(s)?
- Who are you?
- Why should an employer hire you?

This chapter is divided into three parts: Skills Evaluation, Accomplishments Inventory, and a Career Summary. The structure of this assessment chapter will help you find your own answers to the eight questions just listed.

SKILLS EVALUATION

What Can You Do?

If you have a sharp awareness of what you are capable of doing, you already have the potential for success in writing your résumé and in landing the right job. Do you know what your demonstrated strengths are? Your limitations and weaknesses? Which skills need to be improved?

An unblurred vision of what you can do and of what you have to offer is essential for writing an effective résumé and for getting a successful interview.

How can you convey your strengths if you are not clear about them in your own mind? The following exercise can help you identify your skills and evaluate your level of competence. It can also show you your level of enjoyment and interest in using these skills.

> Find out what you like doing best and get someone to pay you for doing it.

If you are "good" at doing something, you probably also enjoy doing it. You will, then, do it more often and get even better at doing it. The reverse is also true: you often dislike doing those things that you are not "good" at doing. One way to find your strengths and weaknesses is to review your previous job-related activities and decide which tasks you enjoyed performing and which ones you kept putting off as long as possible because you disliked doing them.

Your skills and accomplishments are interrelated. Skills you were previously unaware of will be revealed in your Accomplishments Inventory. The reverse is also true: your skills will remind you of other accomplishments that you have not yet identified.

SKILLS EVALUATION WORKSHEET

INSTRUCTIONS: The purpose of this exercise is to discover your level of ability in each skill.

1. Rate your skills using the following key:*
   g = good
   p = poor
2. Enter the appropriate letter in the "LEVEL" column below.
3. Check the third column if you want to use it at work.
4. Add other skills you can do at the end of each section.
5. Be honest with yourself. Your opinion of your abilities does count a great deal. You must admit to what is true about your assets.

INTELLECTUAL/ADMINISTRATIVE

Ability	Level	Want to Use
Organization		
Bookkeeping		
Decision Making		
Editing		
Evaluation		
Logical Organization		
Planning		
Problem Solving		
Program Development		
Policy Formulation		
Research		
Scheduling		
Studying		
Troubleshooting		

*You are either good at this particular skill or you are not. Ultimately you want to know quickly where you excell. The gradations of "fair" and "very good" or "very poor" have proven to inhibit appropriate responses from executives who are humble or too exact for the purposes of this exercise.

SKILLS EVALUATION WORKSHEET *(Continued)*

CREATIVE

Ability	Level	Want to Use
Adapting		
Creating		
Composing		
Designing		
Innovating		
Inventing		
Writing		

MECHANICAL

Ability	Level	Want to Use
Computer Usage		
Building		
Carpentry		
Drafting		
Physical Dexterity		
Repair		
Typing		
Wordprocessing		

SKILLS EVALUATION WORKSHEET *(Continued)*

MANAGEMENT

Ability	Level	Want to Use
Analyzing		
Coordinating		
Controlling		
Directing		
Goal Setting		
Guidance		
Judging		
Leading		
Managing		
Motivating		
Negotiating		
Persuading		
Planning		
Problem Solving		
Promotion		
Selecting		
Supervising		
Teaching		
Training		
Troubleshooting		

SKILLS EVALUATION WORKSHEET *(Continued)*

COMMUNICATION/INTERPERSONAL
Interface with people above/below, internally/externally

Ability	Level	Want to Use
Listening		
Selling		
Speaking		
Rapport Building		
Team Player		
Writing		
Foreign Language (identify)		
Other:		

SKILLS EVALUATION WORKSHEET *(Continued)*

List those skills that you marked GOOD (g) and POOR (p) in the appropriate columns below.

This will give you an indication of your strengths and weaknesses.

Good	Poor*
1.	1.
2.	2.
3.	3.
4.	4.
5.	5.
6.	6.
7.	7.
8.	8.
9.	9.
10.	10.
11.	11.
12.	12.
13.	13.
14.	14.
15.	15.
16.	16.
17.	17.
18.	18.
19.	19.
20.	20.

*If you marked "poor," it could mean that you have no aptitude for that particular skill or that you simply haven't had an opportunity to develop it. Decide which reason is the most likely, because you need to know whether you should avoid situations in which these skills are needed, or whether it is all right to go ahead and seek new experiences that require these skills.

Using Examples as Evidence

For each strong skill you identify (you placed a "good" after it on the Skills Evaluation Worksheet), you should be prepared to explain the skill to a prospective employer by giving a brief example of how such a skill can be used in the job applied for. To help you do this with ease in the interview, write a specific example for each skill listed in the "good" column on the last page of the Skills Evaluation Worksheet. This is not bragging. Rather, it is the way to validate what you say you can do. Use factual examples of what you did and what you learned along the way. Complete the Skills Match Worksheet on pages 86–87 before going on to the next section.

ACCOMPLISHMENTS INVENTORY

What Have You Done?

> The résumé should be an accurate description of a person's track record, with quantitative and qualitative data and described responsibilities and accomplishments.
>
> Partner
> Executive Search Firm
> Denver

Show the employer what you have done before, and he will translate it into what you can do for him. The power of your résumé is in your accomplishments:

- What have you done?
- What were the results?

Results Are What Count

Did you work hard at your job? That isn't enough. Never assume that the reader will know what you mean. State the consequences of your efforts. Remember that most employers are results-oriented.

SKILLS MATCH WORKSHEET

The purpose of this Skills Match Worksheet is to provide an evaluation by matching your skills against the skills required by the targeted job. It is a tool for evaluating how your capabilities match the required skills for each position that interests you. One excellent use is to format each classified ad into a worksheet like this one. This will help you to write a better letter or to have a more successful interview.

1. Write the name of the job title that you would most like to have.
2. Fill out the skills columns (after you have completed the previous SKILLS EVALUATION form).

JOB TITLE (first choice) ______________________________

SKILLS REQUIRED:	MY SKILLS:
1.	1.
2.	2.
3.	3.
4.	4.
5.	5.
6.	6.
7.	7.
8.	8.
9.	9.
10.	10.

SKILLS MATCH WORKSHEET *(Continued)*

JOB TITLE (second choice) ______________________________

SKILLS REQUIRED:	MY SKILLS:
1.	1.
2.	2.
3.	3.
4.	4.
5.	5.
6.	6.
7.	7.
8.	8.
9.	9.
10.	10.

Tell your prospective employer what you can do for him. Capitalize on your skills and experience by using words and numbers that verify results. For example, compare these two statements of achievement:

Job Candidate 1: Responsible for all controllership treasury, MIS, and audit activities for major consumer foods company.

Job Candidate 2: Directed all controllership treasury, MIS, and audit functions for Fortune 500 consumer foods company, five domestic and international subsidiaries, staff of 85, and budget of $10 million.

Which candidate would you believe and want to hear more about? This should be obvious. The second job candidate gives you hard data and uses words that are forceful. In addition, the second candidate demonstrates an understanding of the axiom most managers follow: results must be quantifiable and tangible.

THE SIGNIFICANCE OF YOUR ACCOMPLISHMENTS INVENTORY

Learning how to communicate your accomplishments is essential to a good résumé. First, you must learn what an accomplishments inventory is. Then, you must learn why it is necessary. Here, you will also learn how to take this inventory. It is not a difficult concept, but many executive job seekers either try to take a shortcut or are overcome with anxieties over this portion of the résumé process.

What *is* an Accomplishments Inventory? This is a listing of your completed work. An accomplishment is any activity that you have done successfully. But remember, success must be measured and measurable in terms that are meaningful to the organization.

Although your potential employer will want to know about your titles and responsibilities, the decision to hire you will be based on your accomplishments. Can you increase profits? Can you deliver services or increase efficiency?

You will need your accomplishments list for a constant reference throughout your job search for the following reasons:

- It is the basis for all communication, both written and oral.
- It will prepare you for each interview as you consistently apply these accomplishments to each particular company and position.
- It will serve to validate your self-esteem and rebuild your confidence.

Jeffrey Ryan was the vice president of marketing for a Fortune 500 pharmaceutical company. In his job search, he came across an ad for a marketing executive in a similar but smaller company. The major requirement in the ad was an international marketing background. Ryan had not really considered his background as international because he only had some exposure more than 17 years ago. However, after reviewing his Accomplishments Inventory (which was the result of a thorough brainstorming effort at the onset of his job search), his three months of international experience surfaced. Ryan reviewed these international accomplishments and was then able to write his cover letter and prepare himself for the interview accordingly. Incidentally, Ryan did get the interview and the job. Even though his international experience was not strong, he made use of it as an opportunity to sell himself in the interview.

The first step in the Accomplishments Inventory is brainstorming. If Ryan had not thoroughly searched his memory, his international experience may have been overlooked.

Don't Throw Anything Out

As you develop the inventory of your accomplishments, some will appear absurd or insignificant. Don't worry about this, because each accomplishment has the possibility of being valuable to a potential employer. Put on your list every accomplishment you can remember. You can always condense the list later. You will need to work hard to retrieve these accomplishments from your memory. Allow yourself plenty of time. Immediately before going to sleep, tell yourself that when you wake up, you will remember some new ones. Your subconscious mind will do the work for you during the night. Be sure to keep a pencil and paper on your bedside table in case you wake up at night with a sudden remembrance. If you don't write it down, you may forget it by morning.

This list should be the total of your experience. You will use this list to develop your résumé, to develop an alternative résumé, to write a broadcast letter, to prepare for an interview, and to write a thank you letter.

After the first chronological draft of your accomplishments is completed, go back and edit it three times.

Step-by-Step Directions for Developing the Accomplishments Inventory

1. *Brainstorm.* Use the worksheets in this section to get started. These lists should cover your entire career (paid and unpaid). At this point, don't concern yourself with length.
2. *Edit Number One.* Check for strengths. Be concise and specific. You should be able to use these phrases "as is" in all written communication. Does this accomplishment say what you want it to say? Can this accomplishment be broken down into more than one? Ask yourself these questions for each accomplishment.
3. *Edit Number Two.* Use the action-oriented words list (p. 92) to help demonstrate what you have actually accomplished. Stay away from nondefinite words such as "coordinated." (At the senior level, this is usually a nebulous word.) Eliminate unnecessary words.

4. *Edit Number Three.* Quantify your results (contributions):

   Wrong: Responsible for significant increase in sales volume.
   Right: Increased annual sales volume by $1.8 million.

   If you cannot readily find the needed statistics, make an educated guess, but keep actual figures as your objective.

5. *Label.* Label each accomplishment in the left margin according to function. Accomplishments could have more than one function, such as management, training, and MIS.

   In the sample which follows, the accomplishment could be labeled in any of three areas: management, training, or MIS. You will decide which label to emphasize in your résumé according to what functional area you need to highlight to give credence to your objective.

   > Managed the conversion from a DEC to an IBM system. Directed installation of hardware and software and the training of personnel. Centralized systems. Projected annual savings of $750,000.

6. *Share the Credit.* No one works in a complete vacuum. Give others credit for what they did. If you didn't do it alone, say so. For example:

   > Worked on taskforce to negotiate acquisition of new product line.

This says other things about you that are also important. "Worked on taskforce" . . . tells the reader you are a team player, but at the same time gives you credit for the experience.

As you revise and rewrite the rough draft of your accomplishments, make sure each one meets one or more of the following criteria:

- You contributed to increased profit.
- You made a contribution to efficiency without additional money, time, or personnel.

ACTION-ORIENTED WORDS

The following is a list of action-oriented words. Read through this list, then think of more words to add to it. Refer to this list as you prepare your Accomplishments Worksheet (see pp. 96 and 97).

Accelerated
Achieved
Administered
Analyzed
Built
Conceived
Conducted
Contracted
Converted
Created
Cut
Delivered
Developed
Devised
Directed
Doubled
Drafted
Edited
Eliminated
Established
Evaluated
Exhibited
Expanded

Formulated
Generated
Headed
Implemented
Improved
Innovated
Installed
Invented
Launched
Maintained
Managed
Negotiated
Operated
Organized
Performed
Planned
Prepared
Produced
Programmed
Promoted
Provided
Recommended
Reduced

Reorganized
Researched
Set Up
Simplified
Sold
Solved
Streamlined
Strengthened
Succeeded
Supervised
Supported
Trained
Translated
Trimmed
Tripled
Uncovered
Unified
Unraveled
Widened
Won
Wrote

- You increased productivity.
- You provided services that were a benefit to the organization.
- It was accomplished because you were there.
- It would not have been accomplished had you not been there.
- You simplified a procedure.
- The results were accomplished with the minimum use of resources.
- You used the same resources to achieve additional results.
- A goal was achieved for the first time because of you.
- A goal was reached more quickly because of your work.

Don't Take Yourself for Granted

You have more skills than you realize. As you review your accomplishments, your own individual pattern of skills, abilities, and excellence will surface. Review the following sample accomplishments, but remember:

> The résumé is a vehicle for promoting one's professional accomplishments—keep it complete, brief, and fact-based.
>
> John Bernat
> Director of Personnel
> Rush-Presbyterian Medical Center
> Chicago

- Negotiated the merger of a $67 million company with a Midwestern subsidiary having a related product line. Resulted in a 10 percent increase in market share and a 27.5 percent increase in profit after the second year.
- Established functional divisional organization resulting in a $3 million annual salaried headcount reduction.
- Created new international division spanning all product lines. Hired new international executive vice president and accomplished major reorganization with significant cost reduction. Projected two year savings of $2.5 million.

- Initiated and directed reorganization of North American and European financial groups. Consolidated accounting groups with savings of $500,000. Reduced manpower 18 percent with no loss in productivity.
- Solved equipment problem on a high-tech piece of machinery on customer's site. Obtained recognition for effecting a better level of equipment performance. Resulted in sales contract renewal and the sale of a national service contract of $85,000.
- Reorganized purchasing from scatter plans to centralized purchases. Saved corporation $250,000 annually.
- Developed a Domestic Sales Unit for the corporation. Generated cumulative earnings increase of $3.6 million.
- Instituted tax planning that lowered effective tax rate of corporation by 6 percent in two years through utilization of off-shore subsidiary, research and development credits, and investing in tax-exempt obligations and preferred stocks.

CAREER SUMMARY

Who Are You?

> What is it that is important about you that you want them to know?
>
> Steve Merman, Ph.D.
> Principal
> PMG Incorporated
> Denver-based Outplacement Firm

Be able to describe who you are professionally in two to five sentences. The career summary serves three purposes:

- You will discover whether you are clear about who you are and what you have to offer a potential employer.

- You will discover what your response is to the two most common questions you will be asked: "Who are you?" and "What do you want?" At each step of your job search, in a letter, on the telephone, and in person, you will be expected to answer these two questions in a matter of seconds.
- The career summary is very often appropriate at the top of a résumé instead of the traditional "career objective" section because it gives focus to the résumé while allowing latitude for more job options. Review the following examples:

> *Not Strong Enough:* I am a finance professional and I have worked for several companies. I live in San Francisco and prefer to stay here, if possible. My company is closing operations here. I have had progressively more responsible positions and a 20-year track record in treasury and internal financial management. Responsibilities include all domestic and international finance and administrative functions for the corporate offices. Had dotted responsibilities for subsidiary finance functions. Received "Who's Who Award" for three consecutive years. Received MBA while working full time.
>
> *Stronger:* Finance and Planning Executive with extensive experience in domestic and international treasury, business planning, and analysis. Managed finance and planning functions here and abroad during 20 years with three Fortune 500 companies. Skilled analyst and internal consultant to top management on business plans, investments, and performance.

These two versions of the same financial executive's Career Summary are very different in their respective impact. One is wordy and gives unnecessary information. Which one would you prefer to see come across your desk?

Your Career Summary (sometimes called "Qualifications Summary" or just "Summary") may be your only chance to show the reader your ability to make a worthwhile and valuable contribution. When writing it, you must do the following:

ACCOMPLISHMENTS INVENTORY WORKSHEET
LIST I (Paid)

For each position you have held, identify your accomplishments. Include those accomplishments that were completed under your supervision by subordinates. Begin with the most recent.

As you develop the list, keep this question in mind: What was accomplished because you were there? Also, be sure to include dates, titles, and organizations.

____

____

____

____

____

____

____

____

____

____

____

____

____

____

____

____

____

ACCOMPLISHMENTS INVENTORY WORKSHEET
LIST II (Unpaid)

Organization Membership

List all groups of which you have been a member. Include civic, social, cultural, and professional.

Group	Responsibility	Accomplishments

1. Provide positive statements to encourage the reader to read on.
2. Be concise. Brevity is as important as the strength of the words you select.
3. "Summarize your career progression, stressing your strongest selling points in relation to the type and level of position you are seeking."

    Claudia Gentner
    Vice President
    Seagate Associates
    New Jersey-Based Outplacement Firm

4. Include enough information to give the reader a sense of who you are. Emphasize the following areas:
    - Your functional area(s) of expertise
    - Specific technical expertise
    - Breadth of experience (number of years, if not too long or too short)
    - Rapid career advancement
    - Particular strengths
    - Types of industries in which you have worked, if it helps to sell your qualifications

SAMPLE CAREER SUMMARIES

Review these examples, and then develop your own Career Summary.

Corporate Tax Executive

Key Corporate accomplishments—Attorney and C.P.A. with strong technical and analytical abilities. Highly effective administrator and excellent communicator. Substantial and diversified multinational corporate experience. Extensive planning to comply with and benefit from foreign and U.S. tax laws. Appreciates business and financial impact of tax decisions.

Senior Marketing and Sales Executive

Proven record with accomplishments in formulating marketing strategies, product revitalization, organizational restructuring, improving customer relations, and the development of systems sales strategies for two Fortune 500 companies. Substantial international sales and marketing experience. Able to conceive, develop, and implement marketing strategies that are responsive to customer market needs.

General Management/Marketing Management

Extensive general management and marketing experience, both domestic and international. Excellent record of developing new markets, implementing programs, and rebuilding business sectors. Managed multi-country marketing/sales teams for leading international industrial products firm. Redirected problem lines of business for major financial services company.

Manufacturing Executive

Manufacturing vice president with broad engineering and manufacturing experience and demonstrated accomplishments in cost control, problem resolution, and productivity improvement aimed at bottom line impact. Achieved high-quality standards, cost savings, employee involvement, and high level of customer satisfaction in corporations ranging in size from Fortune 500 to 1000.

General Management

Results-oriented, general management executive with record of accomplishments in operations management. Demonstrated ability to improve productivity and profit. Able to build strong, productive teams. Consistent record of making significant increases in return on net assets employed. Considerable international experience. Demonstrated substantial increases in ROI in startup operations.

By now you should be seeing the results of your efforts and should have a heightened sense of who you are, what you have done, and what you can do. If you don't think you have enough information, or if you are having trouble sorting it out, you may need to seek the help of an objective Career Counselor. (See Chapter 10.)

CAREER SUMMARY WORKSHEET

Instructions: Use the preceding rules and examples to help you create your own short career biography. In addition, the third column in the Cross Over exercise can help you emphasize the parts of your experience that would be the most interesting to your potential buyer.

CAREER SUMMARY:

____

____

____

____

____

____

____

____

____

____

____

____

____

____

____

____

____

____

If you are no longer employed and are conducting a job search without the help of an outplacement firm, go back to your former employer and ask for outplacement assistance before you seek professional counseling or any kind of help. Your chances of receiving help from a past employer are particularly good if you are an older or long-term employee, member of a protected class, or if there are some extenuating circumstances. In my experience, companies are often willing to provide this service when asked.

6

Go: Build the Best Résumé

Appearance is reality.

Anonymous

The objective of this chapter is to help you to build the best résumé possible. You are about to become both the architect and the construction foreman. The architect is a strategist. He listens to his clients, their desires, their needs, and their lifestyles. The construction foreman works closely with the architect to build a good structure that meets the municipal codes and architectural standards.

As you work through this chapter, draw upon Chapters 4 and 5 to help you build the best résumé possible.

> Résumés need to be attractive, directed, concise, and highlight achievement!
>
> A. R. Swayne, Jr.
> Vice President Personnel
> Alberto-Culver
> Franklin Park

Perception is the first truth for the résumé reader. The following case emphasizes the importance of perception.

> Donald Hayes attended Stanford University for 4 years, but he did not receive a degree. He joined the Air Force during his final semester because he wanted to fight in the Vietnam conflict. It bothered Hayes that he didn't get his degree. Résumé screeners called him in for interviews on the assumption that he had his degree. Hayes never lied. He wrote on his résumé the dates he attended Stanford, and he disclosed his major. The dates showed a four-year period. The readers saw Stanford and the four-year time span that people typically take to get their degrees, and he got his interviews. Once in the interview, he had the opportunity to sell himself to get the job. He took the opportunity, and he got his job.

Hayes was not lying. The résumé reader was assuming. This is a perception issue. Don't underestimate the power of perception. It can work for you, or it can work against you.

▶ **Strategy 8:** Pay attention to the smallest detail. Even a misplaced word can be detrimental.

Before the interview is the time to strategize every word. The kinds of words you use, and whether you put a particular word in or leave it out, will influence the reader. One word can effect the perception of the reader either positively or negatively. Use words that are positive, powerful, and forceful. Your résumé must make a positive impact on the decision maker. He reads hundreds of résumés; he needs to be impressed with yours. Your choice of words can make all the difference.

My cup is half full—Infers a positive.

My cup is half empty—Infers a negative.

Cliché or no cliché, this message is loud and forceful. Anything you infer in your résumé's presentation will no doubt effect the reader's perception.

Competition and Distinction

Will your résumé distinguish you from all the other applicants, many of whom will have been coached as well as you? You are definitely competing for the job you want, so make your résumé your mark of distinction.

Use this chapter to learn quick and easy methods for organizing your résumé.

▶ **Strategy 9:** Let your accomplishments rather than your zeal to be noticed set your résumé apart.

PRE-RÉSUMÉ WORKSHEET

You will need this worksheet as a tool to begin putting it all together. Before you begin this worksheet, be sure you have completed your Accomplishments Inventory (Chapter 5).

The Pre-Résumé Worksheet was developed to help provide focus for the résumé. It is meant as a "memory jogger." Because you will be selecting and culling from this worksheet, it forms the basis for your final résumé.

Fill in the blanks. Write down what you know. Use a pencil so that you can make corrections more easily. List all the jobs you have had, all the training programs and colleges you attended, and so on. Later, you can condense it to what is strategically appropriate for your objective and the objectives of your prospective employers.

Most lists of accomplishments are put in order from the strongest to the weakest. However, I have found that it works better to place the weakest accomplishments between the stronger ones. Do this when you get to the Experience segment of this worksheet. Repeat this for each job title.

Use the sections that follow in this chapter to help you complete and refine the worksheet on page 107.

APPEARANCE: HOW YOUR RÉSUMÉ SHOULD LOOK

> "Initial first impression and organization are very important."
>
> Manager Professional Recruitment
> Insurance Company
> Hartford

Decision makers make instant judgments about you from their first reading of your résumé. Their perceptions, true or false, may include the following:

- If your résumé is messy, you could be careless or disorganized about your work.

PRE-RÉSUMÉ WORKSHEET

Position Objective (see Goals Definition in Chapter 2)

Education (list of colleges, majors, degrees, year of graduation, certifications) Do not include high school.

PRE-RÉSUMÉ WORKSHEET *(Continued)*

Training (list courses, conferences, seminars, and training programs that are relevant)

___

___

___

___

___

Career Summary

___

___

___

___

___

Experience (Employment History)

Include paid and unpaid. Depending on the format you choose, you may find it helpful to copy this information directly from the Accomplishments Inventory you have already completed. List in reverse chronological order. This history of your employment is the basis of your résumé(s). Include the following information for each job:

Make sure the strongest accomplishments are at the beginning and end and the weakest in the list are in the middle.

—Responsibilities (budget, staff, function, etc.)
—Most significant accomplishment
—Next best accomplishment
—Weak accomplishment (of all those worthy of mentioning here)
—Next best accomplishment
—Next best accomplishment
—End with a strong accomplishment

PRE-RÉSUMÉ WORKSHEET *(Continued)*

Dates* Company Name*

Title*

*Insert this heading for each position.

PRE-RÉSUMÉ WORKSHEET *(Continued)*

Professional Activities (associations and societies, including offices held)

____

____

____

____

____

Community Activities (organizations, volunteer work, boards, committees, offices held)

____

____

____

____

____

Honors and Awards (also verbal commendations, if major)

____

____

____

____

Military Experience (branch, highest rank, special training, duties)

____

____

____

____

PRE-RÉSUMÉ WORKSHEET *(Continued)*

Professional References (Do not include on résumé.) It is important to identify these early. List three to five references with company, title, address, and telephone number. Make certain these are the good references you believe them to be.

1. Name ______________________________

   Title ______________________________

   Company ______________________________

   Address ______________________________

   Telephone ______________________________

2. Name ______________________________

   Title ______________________________

   Company ______________________________

   Address ______________________________

   Telephone ______________________________

3. Name ______________________________

   Title ______________________________

   Company ______________________________

   Address ______________________________

   Telephone ______________________________

4. Name ______________________________

   Title ______________________________

   Company ______________________________

   Address ______________________________

   Telephone ______________________________

- If your résumé is cluttered, you did not take the time to condense it into specific information.
- If your résumé is too long, you presume the interviewer has lots of time to waste.
- If your résumé has typos or poor grammar, you are either careless about detail or illiterate (or both), and you did not take the time to proofread and edit.
- If your résumé is gimmicky or cute, you are not professional. You may also be insulting and presumptuous.
- If your résumé is difficult to read because the type is too small, or it is too cluttered, or it does not have enough white space, the reviewer might decide to discard it.
- If your résumé is typeset, you may be sending out hundreds of them.

The résumé reader is in a hurry. He typically reads many résumés at night because of a tight schedule during the day. Fatigued, this recruiter wants to get through his task and relax. A first scan is too often the permanent perception. You cannot take the chance. Use the guidelines that follow to make your résumé easy to read.

> I look at a volume of résumés for each open position, so "scanning" is my first cut. Make the highlights of your career grab my attention on the first cut. Market yourself.
>
> Judith A. Harper
> Manager Human Resources
> McCormick & Company, Inc.
> Hayward

GUIDELINES FOR RÉSUMÉS

Paper

Use white bond paper (25 lb rag is recommended). If you prefer color, stay with ivory (cream/buff).

Size

Always use 8½ × 11 inch paper. Some experts recommend legal size or slightly smaller than 8½ × 11 as alternatives. However, I recommend that you stay with the standard size because if it is too big, it could be awkward to handle and file, and if it is too small, it could get lost.

Typing/Word Processing

It is very important that your résumé be free of errors. Proofread it at least three times after the final draft. I recommend that you also have two others proofread this final draft. Use an electric typewriter for a clear, clean copy, or use a good letter-quality printer if you use a word processor. The word processor is easier because corrections and additions can be made with ease at any time.

Duplication

The offset process is recommended because it presents a clean, clear copy for a small amount of money. Do not use photocopies or carbon copies.

Underlining and Capitalization

Do not overdo these! The reason for underlining and capitalization is to highlight important points. However, if overdone, the résumé becomes more difficult to read.

Boldface or Italic

You can use boldface or italic if it is done on a good printer. As with underlining and capitalization, use sparingly.

Spacing

For clarity, leave ample spacing on all four margins, and lots of white space in the résumé itself. This cannot be overemphasized.

Name Change of Former Employer

Write the present name first, then, immediately following, write the former name parenthetically. Use this as an example: United Can Company (formerly known as Cutler Can, Inc.).

Abbreviation/Industry Jargon

Résumés should be written so as to be easily understood by a non-technician. Spell every word (including titles). College degrees are the only words that may be abbreviated. You cannot assume that the reader knows your industry acronyms or jargon. An exception is abbreviations or acronyms that are universal, such as MIS for management information systems.

Consistency

Use either full sentences or incomplete sentences; never use both. My recommendation is to use incomplete sentences that begin with an action verb. This seems to be the most commonly accepted form. Stay away from "I did this, and I did that."

Length

Your résumé must not exceed two pages. After writing all that you can possibly write, you must then condense it to one or two pages. It can *always* be done, no matter how long your résumé draft is. You will be able to distinguish what is important from what is not important after you use the Cross Over Strategy (Chapter 3).

Current Résumé

Do not send a résumé that has your most recent experience typed (or handwritten) onto an old, photocopied résumé.

You Are the Author of Your Résumé

Why should you write your own résumé? Résumé services are appropriate for helping you with typing, word processing, and information. However, using such agencies for career counseling is not recommended.

When you buy a résumé service, sometimes your personal accomplishments are written into a canned format. This kind of résumé writing may not portray you at your best. It is better to write it yourself.

CONTENTS: A REVIEW OF WHAT A RÉSUMÉ SHOULD CONTAIN

> "A résumé should talk about accomplishments."
>
> Recruitment Manager
> Major Bank
> New York

What should you include in your résumé?

- Do you mention that you are married and have two children?
- Do you write down your board membership in your local church?
- Do you tell why you left your last employer?
- Do you write in the nine-month job that didn't work out?

This section reviews these questions and others. It cannot be overemphasized that your résumé must be a carefully crafted document. What may be important for someone else to include could be disastrous for you.

> Janet Innes is a candidate for a vice president of finance position for a Fortune 500 industrial firm. She has worked her way up through her career ladder in two other companies. Twenty-five years ago, she spent two years teaching junior high school.

Does Innes include those two years of teaching on her résumé? Unless she has a very good reason for doing so, I say "No." The reader could concentrate on the teaching experience and could have difficulty seeing Janet Innes as anyone else but a teacher, even with all those good years of finance-related experience.

Usually, the following topic areas are included in a résumé. However, if the topic is not applicable to the individual's background, it should be left out.

- Personal information
- Career summary (qualifications)
- Education/training
- Experience (employment history)
- Professional activities
- Community activities
- Honors and awards
- Military experience
- References

You will need to research the following information:

Position Objective

Leave this subject for your cover letter. Write your position objective here only to keep your thoughts goal-directed. In general, it should not be included in the résumé itself because it could limit the use of your résumé or the options otherwise available to you. (See Goals Definition worksheet, p. 16.)

Personal Information

Leave out anything that might be misconstrued or superfluous (see section on Résumé Don'ts, p. 128). Include only: Name, Address, Telephone number(s).

Education/Training

This can be near the top of your résumé or at the end, depending on the power of your particular educational credentials. If you do not have a college degree, put your educational information at the end or leave it off the résumé entirely. If your credentials add strength because of your major or where you went to school, you might decide to place it at the top of the first page.

Career Summary

Write any major strengths (skills) here. A few words to a few sentences is sufficient. (See Career Summary in Chapter 5.) Use this qualification summary rather than a written position objective. This summary statement can help clarify your focus for the reader. It also helps you to avoid the possible dangers inherent in a statement of your objective.

All résumé readers want to know your objective. Your résumé should be focused enough without resorting to writing a specific objective statement. Your résumé could be rejected because of either a too narrow or a too general objective statement. The following comparison between a summary and an objective statement will illustrate the difference:

> *Summary:*
> Eighteen years of steadily increasing production management accomplishments with two Fortune 1000 corporations. Strong experience and qualifications in operations management, product manufacturing, cost estimating and controls, budget forecasting, and manufacturing engineering. Particular strengths in start-up and turnaround situations.
>
> *Objective:*
> To obtain a challenging production management position commensurate with the education and business experience I have acquired.

The summary statement gives you latitude. If there is not a senior production management position available at this time, your summary could open other options to you within this organization. The objective statement is potentially dangerous for two reasons: First, the word "challenging" is overdone and ill-defined; second, production management alone could be limiting. If the position they have open is in manufacturing engineering, you may be discarded because the reader did not read on to find this particular capability identified.

Experience

This includes paid and unpaid. Use the Action-Oriented Words list on p. 92 to develop and write your inventory of accomplishments. (See Chapter 5.)

The format you ultimately use depends on your particular background. (See following section.)

Professional Activities

These can include papers or presentations, organizations (as member, officer, etc.), publications, committees, and conferences or seminars (as attendee or worker). Include only those activities that relate to your target objective.

Community Activities

If the activity is related or appropriate to your career objective, include it. For example,

> Non-Partisan League of Voters, Healthcare Committee, chaired committee and wrote a study on the status of healthcare in developing nations.

This activity is appropriate for your résumé if your objective is in the healthcare field or requires a writing skill.

Honors and Awards

Include these only if they are timely or appropriate. If you have been out of college for 20 years, your college awards would normally be too old to be of real value. If a newer award relates specifically to your field or job objective, it should be included.

Military Experience

Include this if you were an officer. Remember to include your accomplishments. If you were enlisted, include only if necessary to account for gaps in employment.

References

"Available upon request" is an appropriate line on your résumé if you have space for a reference section. You will need to produce references eventually, so be sure to ask permission beforehand. Make certain your references know you professionally and can verify your competence. Tell them you will provide their names only in response to a request from a prospective employer or executive recruiter.

FORMAT

> Dates are a must for résumés—most interviewers have been burned too many times by résumés with no dates; then we learn of two jobs in the last six months . . ."
>
> Joe Taylor
> Manager Professional Placement
> Pfizer, Inc.
> New York

There are several types of résumés. For our purposes, we will discuss the three most universally appropriate:

- Chronological
- Functional
- Combination

Chronological

This format is a listing of all jobs, beginning with the most recent. It is the most common and is the easiest to read. If you have not had employment gaps, and if you held successively more responsible positions, this format can show your continuous and upward career growth. The disadvantages are that this format will emphasize each job (positions that no longer interest you or the reader), and that it cannot highlight skills with the kind of emphasis the other formats provide. Although this is the most preferred résumé format, if it absolutely does not work for you, don't use it.

> Jeff O'Malley worked in human resources for 15 years. His last position was the vice president of management staffing for the Healthcare Products Division of one of the world's foremost healthcare/pharmaceutical companies. He left his position to join an outplacement firm four years ago. Recently, he made the decision to go back inside the corporation. He developed a chronological résumé, and on the surface it looked like a winner. His background prior to outplacement was limited to recruiting and some training. This résumé showed outplacement as his predominate experience. How many outplacement positions are there within a corporation anywhere in the corporate community? Decidedly few. He reformatted his résumé. A change to a combination résumé became imperative for O'Malley.

Functional

The emphasis in a functional résumé is on experience, skills, and accomplishments. Major functions or skills are listed with specific accomplishments identified below each topic (see sample functional résumé, p. 138–141). The focus on skills and accomplishments and the ability to hide a void in one's previous employment are definite advantages.

The very general picture of one's work experience and the lack of specific data are disadvantages of the functional format. The biggest problem with using this format is that it does not contain any dates. Sometimes even the names of employers are missing. That is why the functional is easily suspect. This is the least popular format because it suggests that you are covering up.

Combination

This type of résumé is a mixture of both the chronological and the functional. The advantages outweigh the disadvantages of the functional approach described above. It combines the flexibility of the functional résumé with the specifics of the chronological. If the chronological does not work for you, this would be the next best approach.

> Norman Nayson spent the last 18 months as senior vice president of marketing and merchandising for a well-known retailer where he had spent his entire career. At the time, there was a down-turn in the retail industry, and opportunities in his field were few. We structured his résumé to emphasize his marketing accomplishments rather than a chronological history of his career progression. We then developed two résumés. One emphasized his accomplishments in the retail field. In the other, we used the combination format and made the retail experience read more generically: we replaced the name of the company with a description of the size . . . "A division of a Fortune 100 corporation . . . ."
>
> Nayson's résumé was so well-constructed that the interviews were plentiful. He landed a job rather quickly as a senior level marketing executive, even with his limited experience in marketing.

Never alienate the reader with the suggestion that you are covering up. Use the chronological format if it works for you. If it doesn't, use the broadcast letter (discussed in Chapter 7) or the combination format. Resort to the functional when you have no other choice. The following section will give additional clarity and direction.

▶ **Strategy 10:** Use the other formats only when the chronological does not work for you.

HOW TO HANDLE PROBLEMS UNIQUE TO YOUR BACKGROUND

> It has been said that every problem is an opportunity turned inside out.
>
> George Odione, Ph.D.

Nearly every client I have worked with has had a problem or issue to confront in his or her job search: too old, too young, too little experience, and so on.

Interestingly, when we first begin to work together, my clients begin their job searches believing they are alone with this particular problem. They're wrong. They are not alone and you are not alone, because everyone has a problem to overcome in his or her search for the best job.

Here are some guidelines for minimizing the common problems job seekers face.

Older

In the corporate community, youth is more valued than experience (except for the few opportunities available in the executive suite). What to do? Develop a chronological résumé, but only list the last 20 to 25 years. Omit the other years from your résumé. Don't disclose dates for any experience beyond 25 years. Remember to delete the dates in the education section. A second solution is a broadcast letter. The last resort is a functional résumé that only identifies your accomplishments.

Coming Out of the Military, Government Service, or Education to Enter Private Industry

This situation presents issues similar to those facing the typical career changer. Identify your accomplishments as they would relate to the position and industry you are pursuing. Avoid language that is related to the situation you are leaving.

Changed Jobs Frequently

First, try grouping some jobs together under general headings, as in the functional format. A second option is to use a broadcast letter that identifies your accomplishments without identifying company names and dates.

Experience Does Not Directly Relate to the Targeted Position

Use general business terminology rather than words that are specific to your past. Try to use accomplishments that relate as closely as possible to the position you are seeking. In this case, a broadcast letter or a functional résumé are preferred. If need be, you can use generic titles in your résumé to help defer their specific nature. Always tell the truth; however, you can use different terminology to do that.

Totally Lack Experience in the Targeted Area

Use accomplishments that indicate you are a person who possesses drive and a high degree of intelligence that can compensate for your lack of specific experience. Any previous career and/or responsibility change should indicate that the change was successful. Show that you are a quick learner and that you are highly motivated. Learn everything you can about the targeted company, then use that information to build your résumé and to be successful in your interview.

Gaps in Your Employment History

A functional résumé or broadcast letter is usually best. However, first try to use a combination résumé; either leave out the dates or group two or three positions together. If you accomplished something specific during these gaps—something that would be of value to the employer—do not hesitate to reveal it.

Overqualified

This is the most common reason for the decision maker rejecting a résumé after the first glance. Overcome her objections. She may think you would be bored or that you would leave if a better opportunity surfaced. Or, perhaps she may have a younger person in mind. Minimize your strengths by deleting the achievements that could present you as too strong or overpowering (threatening). If the jobs you want do not require the credentials you have, leave out your advanced degrees.

Not Enough Education

Do not be overly alarmed. Unless you are in certain professions, educational requirements can be more flexible than you would imagine. The M.B.A. is, almost without exception, in the specifications required for executive job openings. The greater percentage of senior talent today does not have this credential, but they do get the job if they are able to present their experience as equal to the credential. I have even had a few executive outplacement clients obtain good positions with no degrees.

Missing Skills

Talk about the skills you have. Look for ways to relate what you have done to what your customer wants. Use words that are truthful and make sense to your target audience. Much of what you have done would be difficult to describe as a specific skill, but as an accomplishment, it illustrates that you are capable of doing the job.

A Job in Another City

Looking for a job in another part of the country is more difficult, but it can be done. Organization is very important. You must be persistent in your efforts. The following tasks are absolute necessities:

- Network by long distance
- Arrange telephone interviews
- Arrange well-orchestrated visits to targeted areas

Use the people you know in your home town to connect you with people they know in the new city. Lawyers, bankers, realtors, family members, colleagues, and friends are only a beginning. (See Chapter 9 for more ideas.) If you cannot get a letter of introduction, write one yourself. Tell them what you want, who you are, and when you will contact them for a telephone interview.

The telephone is a cost-efficient device for getting acquainted and asking for a face-to-face informational interview. The library has excellent directories and telephone books for identifying potential employers. Your nearest business reference librarian can become a key source of information. Subscribe to the major newspaper of the city where you want to work. Identify the local chapters of your professional associations. Contact the key executives. They probably have a local membership directory, and may even have a list of job openings in your targeted city.

Plan an extended visit of the city. You should do this weeks, or even several months, in advance. Arrange as many interviews as possible before, during, and after office hours and also on the weekends, if at all possible. If you use your time and money wisely, you should be able to remain in the city until you have accomplished your goals.

Choose Your Best Shot

Don't select a format until you know it is the right one for you. What works for someone else, even with a similar background and career objective, may not be appropriate for you. You must be certain that your selection is based on your own needs. Consider the following examples:

> Jim Sanders has been with smaller, obscure companies. However, he has had progressively more responsible positions. His

most recent position as senior vice president of administration at Varang Corporation is critically important. He reports to the president and the CEO. He plays a key role in the organization's strategic plans.

Bill Smithson is also a senior administrative executive, but at first glance, his titles are less than impressive. He is presently at a senior level at one of the largest divisions of a Fortune 500 industrial firm. His title is Senior Operations Consultant. Although his companies have been world class, his position titles infer a lesser story.

Even if Sanders and Smithson have had other similar experiences, such as the same degrees from colleges of similar reputations, their résumé formats should not be entirely alike. One should highlight his positions, and the other should give greater attention to his companies. Both must stress accomplishments.

RULES OF THE GAME: DO THIS! DON'T DO THAT!

You are the résumé.

Robert A. Marciano
Manager Staffing & Development
Black & Decker Corporation
Towson

Many conflicting opinions have been published on how to write a résumé. These suggestions and rules have been written with good intentions. The experts want to help make résumé preparation easier and more effective, but there is so much advice available that it is easy to become frustrated and confused.

When I work with an executive, I tell him or her, "This is the guideline; here is my rationale . . . If you strongly disagree, tell me why. We can discuss it. Perhaps you have an excellent strategy that specifically fits you and your objective. With whatever you do, there are risks. If you strongly believe that what you intend to do feels right for you, even though it is not according to one of my recommendations, you may decide to take that risk. If so, be sure that you are making a well-informed decision by thoroughly reading this section.

In this book, I give you the best knowledge and advice that I can. Some of the advice may appear to be contrary to what other books and advisors have said. However, this advice is based on the 37-year collective experience of professionals in this field and includes the current research from both a geographic and demographic perspective. These rules work. We have the results to prove it.

Résumé Do's

1. Make your résumé results-oriented; verify (use numbers to validate whenever possible) the payoff to the organization.
2. Stress accomplishments (tell what you did, not what you were responsible for).
3. Be sure to give a short synopsis of your previous employers' vital statistics. (If the organization's size, sales volume, or type of industry/products adds power to your credentials, use them.)
4. Tell the truth: Don't say anything that is untrue. The world is smaller than you might think. Once you are found out (even if you have already started the new job), you may be terminated. One executive said he had an M.B.A. After he began work, the references didn't check out. He was fired. Ironically, the company liked him so much that they would have hired him even without that revered credential.
5. Avoid exaggerations. Be careful how you use numbers. They can be noticed too easily.
6. Avoid being cute or gimmicky. You are not best represented by a document that looks like a menu, a brochure, or a

booklet of cartoons. I have seen such résumés from job seekers who genuinely thought they were being creative.

7. Emphasize your strengths. Concentrate on your most recent positions and accomplishments. Most of the detail should be from the last 10 years of experience. Decrease the detail as you move backwards in your career history.
8. Provide only the essential information. Give the reader enough to make him or her want more.

> Paul Johnson had a 20-year history of achievements in sales and marketing with two premier companies. He listed the same type of achievement six times in three separate position headings. By the sixth appearance, the reader was bored. Johnson should have used the space on his résumé for other achievements and results.

9. Use factual illustrations to demonstrate your ability to solve problems. Use strong verbs and quantify when appropriate. For example,

> Identified lag in accounts receivable. Developed a cash discount for early payment. Reduced days outstanding from 32 to 18. Reduced credit department man-hours by 25 percent.

10. Proofread your résumé at least three times. Wait 24 hours before giving it a final proofing.
11. Ask two other people to critique your résumé. Ask for a critique on style and content.
12. Test market: Make 10 photocopies and use with people you trust enough to ask for an honest evaluation. Use this input to finalize your résumé.

Résumé Don'ts

1. Don't tell how great you are. The results of your work (your worth to the organization) should stand on its own merits.

2. Don't try to take all the credit. It is appropriate and good business sense to share the credit, as in the examples below:

    As a member of the acquisition task force . . .
    Worked with Chairman of the Board to . . .

3. Don't disclose salary on your résumé or cover letter. Try to delay this discussion until the end of the face-to-face interview. Your goal should be to keep them guessing until your talks become serious.
4. Don't include any information that isn't specific to your career objective.
5. Don't include names and ages of children.
6. Don't include leisure time activities (unless they have specific relevance).
7. Avoid irrelevant words and phrases.
8. Omit using the same word more than once in a sentence or paragraph.
9. Don't include reasons for job change.
10. Omit any references to height, weight, health, race, religious affiliation, or family background.
11. Forget your photograph. This is one of the biggest *faux pas* of all.
12. Don't consider the résumé to be the total of your job-search campaign.

RÉSUMÉ WRAP-UP

This section will help you review and control. Using a checklist will help you to be sure you have done your homework. The Résumé Log provides a tool for staying on top of how you use your résumé and how effectively it is working for you.

▸ **Strategy 11:** Manage the ways you use your résumé with the same diligence you used to develop it.

The questions on this checklist are basic to the success of your résumé. Have you done your homework? Can you answer yes to all these questions? If so, you are ready to begin your job search activities in earnest!

RÉSUMÉ CHECKLIST

☐ 1. Did you gather all the data you need?

☐ 2. Did you write out your Objective(s)?

☐ 3. Did you complete the Cross Over Strategy?

☐ 4. Did you spend all the time you need to develop an Accomplishments Inventory?

☐ 5. Did you edit all the raw data for an initial draft?

☐ 6. Did you use the strongest words?

☐ 7. Did you use numbers wherever appropriate?

☐ 8. Did you select the best and most appropriate data?

☐ 9. Did you select the best format for you?

☐ 10. Did you test market your résumé in final draft form?

Résumé Log

The Résumé Log on page 132–133 is a simple record-keeping device. It allows you to keep track of your résumé and its effectiveness during your job search. Remembering who you sent your résumé to can be confusing; this worksheet provides a reference guide and update. Use this sample or modify it to suit your needs. The important thing is to develop some form of control.

SAMPLE RÉSUMÉS

There are two examples under each format. Please keep in mind that these résumés have been reproduced to fit the constraints of our book page. In preparing your résumé be sure to follow the recommendations made in this chapter regarding spacing and format.

1. *Chronological Format* (pp. 134–139)
   General management candidate with no graduate degree
   Dual background both in general management and finance
2. *Functional Format* (pp. 140–143)
   Marketing and public relations executive; listing of skills by topic in Summary section
   Companies identified with no dates given
3. *Combination Format* (pp. 144–149)
   Senior partner in professional firm; titles and dates at top
   Senior human resource executive; companies and dates at end

RÉSUMÉ LOG

Company Name, Address, Telephone	Individual's Name and Title	Date/Directions for Follow-Up

Date/Comment	Date/Final Comment or Follow-Up

Chronological Format 1

ROBERT F. MILLS
23 SENIOR WAY
BIG CITY, COLORADO 80222
(303) 555-5555 (Residence)
(303) 555-1212 (Business)

QUALIFICATIONS SUMMARY

Take charge General Management executive who brings pragmatic insights and solutions to meet profit objectives. Twenty-two years of broad, in-depth experience with technical and managerial achievement in P & L, acquisitions, public offerings, restructuring, divestitures and turnarounds. Achieved projected 140% increase in profit on sales increase volume of 17%.

PROFESSIONAL HISTORY

1985-Present ZENITH AUTOMOTIVE, Division General Motors, Inc.
President and Chief Operating Officer

- Reduced average net assets employed by 18%, resulting in a projected improvement of 84% within two years.
- Shut down two plant facilities and thirteen field warehouses within eighteen months, lowering breakeven unit volume by 16%. Divested three product lines.
- Formulated manpower reduction programs which eliminated 260 out of 1,500 divisional personnel in 18 months. Resulted in a 17% cost reduction.
- Implemented effective cost reduction and productivity improvement programs within a second major product line resulting in a 53% increase in production.
- Launched major part number reduction and consolidation programs resulting in approximately 3% and 8% reduction in two product lines.
- Substantially improved cashflow through reduction of inventories, while maintaining customer service levels at 97%.
- Directed the implementation of divisional plan productivity improvement programs, including closed loop materials requirement planning, quality circles, Kanban system (just in time inventory) and Kaizan systems (zero maintenance).
- Established functional divisional organization resulting in a $3 million annual salaried headcount reduction.
- Created new international division spanning all product lines. Hired new international Executive Vice President and accomplished major reorganization with significant cost reduction.

1963-1985 MOLINE FEDERAL CORPORATION, Southfield, Michigan

1982-1985 Group Vice President
Bearing Replacement Group

- Directed planning, engineering, manufacturing and original equipment sales of two product lines, with full profit and loss responsibility ($230 million sales, 3,500 people, five plants, and one R & D facility).

1976-1982 Vice President, General Manager

- Full profit and loss responsibility with authority for divisional strategic planning and implementation.
- Directed market planning and sales to replacement market customers in the automotive, industrial and heavy duty channels of distribution, plus selected national accounts. Generated increases of 15% in first year.
- Created a separate heavy duty sales division. Resulted in a sales increase from $5.6 million to $28 million in four year period.

1974-1976 Director, Corporate Planning and Development
(Reported to Chairman of the Board)

- Directed the preparation, consolidation and presentation of strategic plans for all groups and divisions within the corporation. Led all corporate divisions in business analysis, plus market and product segmentation studies. Conducted corporate acquisition and divestiture analyses.

1973-1974 Acting General Manager
Plastic Products Division

- Reorganized and restructured plant operations; achieved only year of division profitability during long recession.

1963-1973 Plant Manager Peoria, Illinois
Plant Superintendent
Material and Quality Control Manager
Shift Superintendent
Plant Metallurgist

1960-1963 CATERPILLAR DES MOINES TRACTOR GROUP, Des Moines, Iowa
Plant Metallurgist
Staff Metallurgist

EDUCATION
BS Metallurgical Engineering, 1960, University of Illinois/Champaign

Chronological Format 2

JOHN R. HALL
12 COUNTRY CLUB ROAD
GLEN FOREST, WISCONSIN 53120
(414) 555-5555 (Residence)
(414) 555-1212 (Business)

PROFESSIONAL SUMMARY

An accomplished senior executive with outstanding credentials and a proven record of results. Consistently maintained diligent eye to growth in productivity and bottom-line profitability.

KEY ACCOMPLISHMENTS

1978-Present CANNON METAL PRODUCTS CO., Racine, Wisconsin

Vice President/General Manager (1981-Present) of this manufacturer of high quality hand tools. Responsible for all aspects of manufacturing, purchasing, corporate planning, financial management, MIS, operations and employee relations in five manufacturing facilities as well as union contract negotiation and grievance arbitration.

- Increased inventory turns 60% by eliminating slow moving items, standardizing parts and reducing lead times.
- Successfully reduced back orders from 40% to less than 10%.
- Instituted a computerized inventory report for use by sales, order entry, materials control and manufacturing operations.
- Successfully secured all patent rights to manufacture and distribute a new concept quick release ratchet screwdriver, projected to increase sales by $375,000.
- Negotiated contracts with four unions at terms favorable to management; grievances filed have decreased by 75%.
- Designed and instituted a "no-fault" absenteeism program which effectively reduced absenteeism to less than 2%.
- Served as Co-Chairman of Board of Trustees for Consolidated Industrial Union pension plan; doubled employee pension benefits with no increase in cost to employees.

Chief Financial Officer And Director (1978-1981) Responsible for all financial operations including P & L, administration, cost and general accounting, budget preparation and compliance, credit reporting, bank liaison, financing, as well as direct managerial control of all MIS, costing and credit functions.

JOHN R. HALL
PAGE TWO

- Designed and implemented a "responsibility accounting" system, including a new chart of accounts, as well as computerized general ledger and financial statements.
- Renegotiated all bank financing, reducing interest rates by 0.5%.
- Instrumental in the installation of a LIFO inventory system with a current reserve in excess of $3 million.
- Implemented a direct deposit computerized payroll system.
- Instituted self-insurance for workmen's compensation, resulting in annual savings in excess of $200,000.

1967-1977 DELOITTE, HASKINS & SELLS & CO., Chicago, Illinois

Audit Manager for this Big 8 public accounting firm. Responsible for liaison with both public and private client companies including overseeing all facets of annual audits, financial reporting, acquisition studies, corporate and individual income tax return preparation, systems evaluation, and numerous other functions including the supervision and training of over 75 accountants.

- Chosen to participate as company-wide instructor in such areas as tax and audit training programs.

EDUCATION

CPA, Illinois, 1967
BBA, Degree in Accounting, University of Illinois, 1966

Numerous courses, seminars and workshops including technical seminars for Deloitte, Haskins & Sells & Co.

REFERENCES AVAILABLE UPON REQUEST

Functional Format 1

RONALD ROYCE
26 BERRY LANE
GOOD CITY, NEW JERSEY 07007
(201) 555-5555 (Residence)
(201) 555-1212 (Business)

SUMMARY

Strategy and Planning	Marketing Communications
Financial Relations	Editorial Services
Media Relations	Public Affairs
Community Relations	Management Communications
Meeting Management	Internal Communications
Special Events	Audio Visuals
Public Speaking	Media Training

ACHIEVEMENTS

Administrative Management—Directed corporate staff of 20 with departmental budget of $1.8 million. Conceived and sold to senior management a communications department reorganization, cut expenses $250,000. Consolidated and telescoped over 50 publications and services into a 50% more cost-effective package.

Strategy and Planning—Working with senior management, recommended and implemented company's first full-scale communications program in ten years, involving multiple city, multi-media presentations. Introduced medium of videotape. Recommended and implemented long-range image building program.

Media Relations—Directed new market strategy for major business expansion program; neutralized hostile labor sentiment and created favorable corporate and consumer climate. Worked with trade press and business media to introduce new products and services. Directed and participated in issue-oriented cross-country media tours.

Internal Communications—Conceived and implemented innovative upward communications programs during critical turnaround period. Supervised the writing and production of annual reports, magazines, and newsletters. Reduced publication costs by 35%, while improving impact, quality. Wrote union avoidance communications, resulting in successful company campaigns.

Public Affairs—Initiated government relations program for new plant location. Directed aggressive legislative public relations

RONALD ROYCE
PAGE TWO

campaign to position organization more favorably. Handled constituent inquiries on behalf of White House, Member of Congress, and Department of Defense.

Corporate Communications—Researched, directed, and implemented new logotype and corporate identity program. Authorized and supervised major cost-effective communications audit. Centralized subsidiaries' public relations programs.

EDUCATION

M.A. Industrial Communications, Boston University, 1969
B.S. Communications, Boston University, 1967

LECTURER

Union College, Cranford, New Jersey
Taught effective oral, written and audio visual communications techniques.

PROFESSIONAL AFFILIATIONS

Public Relations Society of America
International Association of Business Communicators
Boston Press Club

Functional Format 2

MARY A. WARREN
7304 CROWN COURT
LAKE FOREST, ILLINOIS 60071
(312) 555-5555 (Residence)
(312) 555-1212 (Business)

QUALIFICATIONS

General Management/Packaged Goods executive with extensive hands-on domestic and international experience with full P & L responsibility at corporate, regional and country levels for multi-national corporations. Strong operations management. Skilled in new product development and new venture start-up. Experienced negotiator, heavy marketing background, strong team builder.

ACCOMPLISHMENTS

- Re-organized a three divisional subsidiary, doubling sales to $18 million and tripling profits to $2 million.
- Re-structured the marketing operation of a $25 million company resulting in a 65% sales increase and a 35% profit increase.
- Established from scratch a new affiliate producing a profit in the first 18 months and annual sales of $3 million.
- Organized an institutional sales group producing first year sales of $3 million and profits of $500,000.
- Revised a sales and distribution system converting a $1 million a year loss into a profit.
- Dissolved a joint venture turning it into an independent operation with sales of $4 million annually.
- Identified and secured manufacturing and distribution partners in seven overseas countries.
- Initiated new product marketing programs leading to the successful introduction of ten new products.
- Recruited and trained a group of professional managers who have since succeeded to senior management positions.

EXPERIENCE

General Management: 10 years with Quaker Oats Company and G. D. Searle marketing consumer food and pharmaceutical products.

MARY A. WARREN
PAGE TWO

Marketing Management: 15 years with Sara Lee and Johnson & Johnson marketing food products and health and beauty aids.

EDUCATION

MBA Marketing, University of Illinois, Champaign
BA Liberal Arts

(*Note*: This résumé will occupy 1 page on an 8½ × 11 sheet. Here, the constraints of the book page made it occupy two.)

Combination Format 1

JOHN POWELL
4112 APPIAN WAY
GREAT HEIGHTS, NEW YORK 10012
(212) 555-5555 (Residence)
(212) 555-1212 (Business)

PROFESSIONAL HISTORY

ARTHUR ANDERSEN & CO.
San Francisco, California

1979-Present	Partner, Audit Services Department
1972-1979	Senior Manager, Audit
1969-1972	Senior, and Audit Staff

CAREER SUMMARY

Region Head of Audit Services directly responsible for concurrently planning, supervising and administering examinations of financial statements primarily for Fortune 1000 clients. Led new practice development. Identified and developed opportunities to provide additional accounting, tax and services to audit clients in manufacturing, consumer products, pensions and benefits plans, transportation, franchise and not-for-profit.

KEY ACCOMPLISHMENTS

- Managed staff of 230. Responsible for increase in revenue to firm of 40% in the past two-year period.
- Directed worldwide audit of a multi-billion dollar, Fortune 50, manufacturing company with annual fees of approximately $3,000,000.
- Made formal presentations to Board members and senior management on tax reduction and deferral opportunities and other recommendations for cash-flow improvement.
- Corrected historical data and evaluated financial forecasts which considered economic factors, sales volume, price projections, etc. prepared by a major client to justify price increases in excess of those otherwise allowable under Wage and Price Stability Program.
- Visited client locations in several Far East countries, Australia and Puerto Rico to gain better understanding of my client's international operations and long-term business strategy, to resolve accounting issues and to effectively coordinate the worldwide audit.
- Revised multinational client's physical inventory procedures to include sophisticated computerized statistical sampling methods which reduced costs while concurrently improving the overall accuracy and effectiveness of physical inventory.

- Developed and evaluated a survey of financial data using statistical sampling techniques which provided an effective and successful response by a multinational client to a foreign government's anti-trust investigation.
- One of a select group of senior managers chosen for a tour-of-duty in the Accounting Services Department of the National Office. Advised partners throughout the firm on complex, often sensitive, accounting and reporting issues encountered by clients requiring prompt resolution.
- Identified and coordinated computer auditing applications and reviews of sophisticated MIS systems and IBM installations for multi-billion dollar client.
- Worked with multinational client to assist with adoption of LIFO inventory method for foreign subsidiaries which resulted in significant tax deferrals.
- Advised clients on appropriate internal procedures and effective short-cut techniques for implementing new accounting standards on segment reporting, inflation accounting, translations principles, etc.
- Instructed a variety of internal educational courses, principally related to statistical sampling and current accounting and auditing developments.
- Interviewed and assessed candidates for employment and participated in annual evaluations of professional staff to determine promotions and salary adjustments.

PROFESSIONAL AND COMMUNITY CERTIFICATION AND MEMBERSHIPS

Certified Public Accountant—California, 1970

California CPA Society

American Institute of Certified Public Accountants

Colorado CPA Society

United Way of Pasadena, Former Board Member

EDUCATION

B.S. in Accounting with High Honors
University of California at Berkeley, 1969

PERSONAL AND BUSINESS REFERENCES AVAILABLE UPON REQUEST

Combination Format 2

JOSEPH P. JONES
64 EXECUTIVE LANE
GREAT WAY, CONNECTICUT 07007
(203) 555-5555 (Residence)
(203) 555-1212 (Business)

QUALIFICATIONS SUMMARY

Profit oriented human resources executive with demonstrated capacity to achieve results in diverse business and organizational conditions. Experience includes over 16 years of increasing responsibility with three major manufacturing companies.

MAJOR ACCOMPLISHMENTS

Management/Strategic and Manpower Planning

As a senior human resource executive for a Fortune 100 corporation, achieved the following:

- Conceived and directed the integration of strategic human resource planning into the corporate business planning process. Resulted in the streamlining and targeting of human resource programs toward the achievement of a record 11.7% increase in net income.
- Developed and formalized systems and procedures for corporate-wide manpower planning, succession planning, and management development.
- Recruited top level executives. Directed the recruitment of management, professional and technical employees.
- Organized and directed the first corporate employee relocation program. Improved productivity and the acceptance of management job transfers 12%.
- Initiated and directed the development of an in-house computerized employee attitude survey program. Used effectively to resolve morale, communications, productivity, and union organizing problems.

Compensation and Benefits

- Directed development of corporate and divisional executive compensation programs. Resulted in effective and competitive programs which enable the company to attract, motivate, and retain highly qualified management employees..
- Organized and directed a self-insured employee benefits structure, which resulted in corporate-wide savings of over $500,000 annually in insurance company retentions.

JOSEPH P. JONES
PAGE TWO

Employee/Labor Relations

- Conceived strategies and directed campaigns which won over 80% of N.L.R.B. union elections. Directed five successful union decertification campaigns.
- Developed preventive labor relations programs which eliminated all election losses in the last three years.
- As Chief Negotiator, achieved contract terms favorable to management in all labor negotiations with no strike time lost. Twenty-five percent of negotiations involved substantial wage or benefit concessions or "give backs"—reduced labor costs $1.25 million in a single negotiation.
- Solved serious E.E.O./A.A.P. problems. Resulted in settling 85% of charges in favor of the company. With a reserve liability of $3.3 million, conciliated the balance at a cost of less than $6,000 per year.

Training

- Organized, coordinated, and directed 13 corporate and regional training conferences for human resources executives of 42 operating companies nationwide.
- Conceived and directed the development of training courses on the establishment of productivity improvement programs. Documented savings in excess of $1 million in the first year after first two programs.

PROFESSIONAL HISTORY

1973-Present	NABISCO FOODS CORPORATION Corporate Director of Human Resources Corporate Director of Employee Relations Corporate Manager of Employee Relations
1971-1973	UNITED GRAIN COMPANY, formerly known as GLOBE MILLS, INC. Assistant Head, Corporate Labor Relations
1966-1971	UNIVERSAL TUBE AND CONDUIT COMPANY Director of Personnel Personnel Manager Assistant Personnel Manager

EDUCATION

1968 MBA, DePaul University, Chicago, Illinois
1964 BA, University of Wisconsin, Madison, Wisconsin

Part 2

The Executive Game Plan: Getting the Job

7

Tools to Make Job Finding Easier

The harder you work, the luckier you get.

Gary Player, Golfer

In this chapter, we'll discuss two important tools to make your goal of finding a job easier—letters and scorekeeping.

LETTERS

Letters are important to your job search. They can provide additional information not suited to the résumé itself. Some letters accompany the résumé. Others go in place of the résumé. You may send a letter without a résumé, but the reverse is never correct. There are many kinds of letters. For the purposes of this book, the focus is on the ones that are most commonly used. See the end of this section for examples that include:

- Cover letter
- Broadcast letter
- Networking letter
- Follow-up letter
- Thank you letter

Rules and Reminders

> Keep your letters brief.
>
> Director of Staffing & Development
> Fortune 50 Diversified Industrial Firm
> Chicago

The general guidelines for developing your written communication are based on good business sense. For example:

- Whenever possible, your letter should be addressed to a specific individual (name and title).

- One $8\frac{1}{2} \times 11$ inch page is recommended (error free, of course). Thank you letters are sometimes the exception, particularly if you decide to use note- or monarch-size paper.
- Every letter should be written and typed individually; not photocopied, and never typeset.
- Keep all communications brief.
- Be clear about why you are writing the letter.
- Show confidence in the contents of the letter; however, be careful not to sound pompous.
- Don't be apologetic or negative.
- Don't be too wordy or philosophical.
- Never lie.

Writing a letter is a major obstacle for most people, yet this is the easiest part of your job search. Look at the recommended contents and structure shown next. Follow the examples, and keep it simple. Each paragraph is only two or three sentences.

The Beginning Paragraph

Capture the reader's interest: Tell him why you are writing the letter, how you heard about the position, why you want to meet him, or why you have selected his company.

The Middle Paragraph

Connect your background to the reader's needs. Summarize the highlights of your experience and, if appropriate, tell how these accomplishments relate to the position. Explain why you think he should meet you.

The End Paragraph

Tell the reader you would like a meeting. You just might get it. However, it is highly recommended that you do not state that you will call him. Too many survey respondents found this approach overly aggressive and presumptuous.

The Cover Letter

A résumé should never be sent without a cover letter. This is your personal introduction to a potential employer. It shows how your experiences and skills match those of a specific position or how you can make a contribution to the company. Your cover letter not only introduces you, it tells the reader what you want. A good cover letter can strengthen a résumé. There are personal characteristics (such as management style), qualities, and career objectives that are not appropriate for the résumé, but that clearly enhance your image when briefly stated in a cover letter.

There are basically three types of cover letters:

1. The executive recruiter
2. The direct mail (to a targeted list of companies)
3. The response (to an ad)

In each case, your letter should be tailored to the situation.

The Executive Recruiter Letter

The executive recruiter letter is written as a courtesy and contains information that should not go in the résumé. The letter should be brief and to the point. However, you don't want to narrow your options by focusing too tightly. This letter requires even more finesse if you have a broad, more diverse background. Always include your current salary. (This is the only type of letter that should include salary information.)

The Direct Mail and the Classified-Ad Letters

These two letters should be addressed (as should all correspondence) to a specific name and title. Be sure this data is correct and current. In the case of a blind advertisement, there is, of course, no way to know name, title, and salutation. The least objectionable is: "Dear Sir or Madam." Omitting the salutation might be a viable solution. Use your best judgment in each situation. Do not list salary data even if requested. If the employer is adamant in the ad about receiving your salary history, you will have to make the decision of whether to go ahead and reveal it.

The Broadcast Letter

There are situations when a broadcast letter is more appropriate:

- Your résumé (even with the accompanying cover letter) may not be specific enough in reference to a particular job goal.
- Your résumé may contain inappropriate information (such as the wrong major or the wrong industry experience).
- You may wish to respond to a blind advertisement and not want the name of your present employer revealed to unknown recipients.

Unlike the cover letter, the broadcast letter is used in place of the résumé rather than in addition to it.

Instructions

Before writing the broadcast letter, it is important to have completed the Accomplishments Inventory list.

This letter, like your résumé, should contain objective measures of job success. For example:

> Negotiated a loan that saved the company $500,000/year interest.

Include a clear and concise inventory of accomplishments with supporting quantitative data. Also include the position and title. For example,

> As Director of Management Information Systems, I developed a computer based inventory control system that reduced inventory by $1,800,000.

The accomplishments of your subordinates belong to your own list of accomplishments because they were done under your responsibility, accountability, and supervision.

Your broadcast letter should pertain to the position you are seeking. You may have two or more broadcast letters if you are seeking more than one type of position.

The Networking Letter

Sometimes called the referral letter, this letter is often used in place of a phone call. There are two types: the first is written by you to request a personal meeting; the second is written on your behalf by someone who knows you professionally, can verify your accomplishments, and is aware of your value. If you know someone who will write a referral letter for you, you are already on the road to success.

You may give a very brief background sketch in the networking letter, but it is not recommended that you enclose a résumé.

The Follow-Up Letter

This letter may be used to confirm an upcoming appointment. It is used as a reminder, and it can also be used to confirm a promise to contact someone on your behalf. This letter can sometimes take the form of a thank you letter. The important thing to remember is that every contact you make should be treated with the greatest of care, professionalism, and courtesy.

The Thank You Letter

▸ **Strategy 12:** Send everyone who helps you a thank you letter, even if their help was minimal.

Everyone who has helped you, whether their help was great or small, deserves a brief typed or handwritten letter of appreciation. Be diligent about this strategy, because this letter will help you in many ways: Your thoughtfulness will be noticed; it will be perceived that you are a person who takes care of details; you will be seen as a person with good interpersonal skills; it will give you a second chance to reaffirm your assets; and, most importantly, it will make the recipient feel good about you and about himself. Send the letter as soon as possible; it is recommended that you send it within three days.

On the following pages, we illustrate the cover letter (p. 156–158), the broadcast letter (p. 159), the networking letter (p. 160–161), the follow-up letter (p. 162), and the thank you letter (p. 163).

KEEPING SCORE

It has been said that to efficiently and effectively reach a major goal, that goal should be broken down into smaller steps. Compare this to the "to do" list used by many executives: as each task is checked off, the larger objective comes closer to reality.

Keeping score enhances confidence and gives a sense of moving forward. The scoreboard can relieve your anxiety over waiting for the phone call, the response letter, or the job offer. Keeping score will also show you which skills you need to practice. The wise executive, as well as the athlete, knows that practice improves the game. You, too, can improve your skills as you play the job-search game. For example, you can improve your telephone techniques by using the phone as a tool again and again; you can improve your résumé and the success of your interviews by continually reviewing the worksheets and advice found in this book; and finally, you can improve your chances of getting the job you want by putting renewed effort into your networking. Your efforts will reward you, and you will win the game.

SAMPLE COVER LETTER:

Executive Recruiter

____
____
____
____

Dear ______________________ :

I have enclosed my résumé for consideration against your client assignments.

My professional background demonstrates an excellent record as general manager in businesses ranging from $17 million to $120 million. I have had major accomplishments in P & L, sales, marketing, and operations. My current compensation is $136,000 plus bonus, car, and perks.

Please feel free to contact me at the above numbers to arrange a mutually convenient appointment.

Sincerely,

SAMPLE COVER LETTER:
Executive Recruiter

____
____
____
____

Dear Mr. Johnson:

As an accomplished chemical executive, I am presenting my qualifications as a candidate for search assignments you may have.

My background involves extensive managerial experience in all phases of the chemical and resin business, including direct management of:

Research & Development—Led the creation of a major line of thermoplastic products.

Sales & Marketing—Improved market share in both up and down business cycles.

Engineering & Operations—Applied practical technology to improve products and processes.

General Management—P & L responsibility for $450 million sales, multi-site operation.

As the enclosed résumé outlines, I have successfully organized the technology and directed the efforts of the many people necessary to develop, produce, and sell a large volume of products for a variety of industrial uses. My solid technical background is coupled with a demonstrated common-sense approach to achieving profitable results. My compensation consists of a base of $98,000 plus bonus of 30%. I would be pleased to further review my background with you.

I look forward to hearing from you.

Sincerely yours,

SAMPLE COVER LETTER:
Classified Ad

____
____
____
____

Dear ________________________ :

In response to your advertisement in The Wall Street Journal for a Senior Vice President of Marketing, I am enclosing my résumé.

For the past four years, I have been the senior marketing officer for a Fortune 100 electronics firm, my thirteen-year career demonstrating increasing responsibility and achievements, two of which include:

- generated $70 million in new business in four years.
- captured $51 million in new market development in three years.

I will be happy to arrange a personal interview with you to further discuss the details of my experience.

Sincerely yours,

SAMPLE BROADCAST LETTER

____
____
____
____

Dear Mr. Shelby:

As the senior operating officer with full P & L responsibility for a major division of a Fortune 100 corporation, I directed all domestic and international units—combined annual sales totaled $800 million. Responsibilities included direction of sales, manufacturing, engineering, finance, legal, and industrial relations to support the product lines that are sold through both wholesale and retail markets.

Your company may have a need for an individual with my background and accomplishments:

- Led major profit turnaround—doubled profits, tripled return on investment, lowered break even 17%, with relatively flat sales volume.
- Directed major productivity improvement programs. Streamlined manufacturing processes. Introduced and installed computer aided design (CAD) systems. Introduced Japanese Kaizan assembly and Kanban inventory systems. Reduced cost of manufacturing $3 million and reduced inventory $12 million.
- Launched six new product lines. Resulted in combined return on new capital investment in excess of 28%. Annual sales of $68 million.
- Closed two major U.S. manufacturing plants and eliminated 11 field warehouses. Reduced fixed costs $4 million. Divested five marginal product lines. Generated $51 million cash.

I graduated from New York University with a B.B.A. in Accounting. I would be happy to discuss my background with you in greater depth.

Very truly yours,

SAMPLE NETWORKING LETTER:
Written by You

____
____
____
____

Dear Mr. Bronson:

I am writing this letter at the suggestion of John Sommers. We serve together on the Junior Achievement Board in Northbrook. John recommended I contact you.

As you may know, the Carton Corporation is closing its Chicago headquarters and nearly all of the corporate staff is being cut. As Director of Finance, I managed all finance, tax, audit, MIS, and controller functions for the corporation. I am now exploring opportunities in the Northeast.

I would like an opportunity for a brief meeting. I realize it is unlikely that you have an appropriate position available at this time. However, I would greatly appreciate your time and advice. I will be traveling to Connecticut in the next few weeks and would very much like to meet you.

Sincerely yours,

SAMPLE NETWORKING LETTER:
Written by Contact

____
____
____
____

Dear John:

Enclosed is the résumé of Joseph Jones. I have taken the liberty of forwarding it to you in the event that his credentials might fit the specifications of one of your existing or upcoming MIS search engagements. I have been associated with Joe for the past four years and know him to be a highly capable individual. We serve together on the United Way Board of Hinsdale. His contributions on the Board and the community have been exceptional.

John, please feel free to contact Mr. Jones directly should you desire further information. Thank you for your consideration.

Best regards,

____
____

WLP/jp
enclosure

SAMPLE LETTER:
Follow-Up

____
____
____
____

Dear ______________________ :

I enjoyed our brief discussion this morning regarding your article in Research and Development News on "Chemical Process Plants in the 1990's."

Thank you for your advice; I look forward to meeting you next Friday at 10:00 a.m. at your Los Robles site. I will appreciate any additional advice and counsel you can provide.

Thank you again.

Very truly yours,

SAMPLE LETTER: Thank You

____

____

____

____

Dear _______________________ :

Thank you again for the opportunity to discuss financial options and opportunities in the Connecticut and Massachusetts area. I sincerely appreciate your good counsel and the time you took to meet with me.

I will be following up on the list of people you gave me. I would like to keep you informed. Again, thank you for your time and your much-valued advice.

Very truly yours,

Here are some suggestions for keeping score.

- Make a scoreboard like the one below for your daily, weekly, and monthly goals.
- List all the steps you need to take to complete each strategy in this manual.
- The sample scoreboard is only a suggested list. Modify it to meet your needs. Make realistic goals for each week, but push yourself, as well.

▸ **Strategy 13:** Keeping score will get you there more quickly.

SAMPLE

Weekly Activity Scoreboard Week of ______________
1. Added __________ names to list of contacts
2. Set up __________ networking meetings with people I don't know
3. Obtained __________ referrals from people I know
4. Attended __________ professional meetings and/or activities
5. Set up __________ meetings with executive recruiters
6. Mailed résumés to __________ executive recruiters
7. Created __________ new ways of getting a job lead
8. Received __________ telephone calls in response to my résumé

Techniques

When . . . people get jobs they sell not only their time and energy but their personalities as well . . .

C. Wright Mills

TELEMARKETING

> Telemarketing is just what the name implies—marketing. You should approach it with the same intensity as you would launch a new product in a major corporation.
>
> Arthur C. Reedie
> Chairman and CEO
> Reedie & Company
> Dallas-Based Outplacement Firm

Successful telemarketing is the result of a good attitude, a high level of energy, a strong commitment, much preparation and practice, and an enormous desire to reach your goals. Your goal, for the purpose of this section, is to arrange a meeting through the use of the telephone.

Call a Personal Contact to Arrange a Networking Meeting

When making this type of call, your only objective is to arrange a brief meeting. It is best to discuss the details and the purpose of the call in person rather than over the telephone, so try to be as vague as possible.

When you do get a meeting with your contact, try to get the names of his contacts so you can meet with them to expand your network.

If your contacts are out of the area, you will need to be more specific as to why you are calling and how the person can help you.

Call a Stranger Without a Referral

Getting yourself ready means doing your homework. Before you pick up the telephone, make certain you know your capabilities and can express them briefly in no more than three sentences. Again, understanding your customer is the key. Find out all you can about the person you are calling. For information and assistance, use your network, as well as the current resources such as directories, newspapers, journals, and associations.

Use the company telephone operator as a source. He may know a great deal more than anyone else, particularly if he has been there for any length of time. The correct spelling of names, the correct title, and contacts at other locations are probably all found in the switchboard operator's directory. Be friendly and appreciative to this vital source and he will increase your knowledge of the company.

Getting Through the Secretary

The higher the level of the person you are calling, the stronger and more protective the secretary will be. Getting past the secretary is an art. Be convincing, confident, and logical. You must sound as if you are in control. Practice and be prepared. If you were referred, use your contact's name. Even better, persuade your referral to make a call to the executive (and his secretary) in advance of your call.

The busy executive you are calling will only want a short and concise conversation. Give only this brief information:

- Your name
- The person who referred you (if appropriate)
- Why you called
- What you want (a meeting)

Adapt your personal style to his or hers. After you get the appointment, immediately write a short letter to thank him/her and to confirm the appointment.

If your telephoning is not going well and you feel discouraged or depressed—STOP. Your negative energy can be felt on the other end. If you don't feel confident, you won't sound confident.

Practice a number of scenarios with a friend. Think out all the possible dialogues and write them down before calling.

When you have a successful day . . . that is, you are getting through and making appointments . . . keep going. Don't stop until you are tired and losing energy, because at that point your mind will lose its sharpness and you will probably begin to sound negative.

▸ **Strategy 14:** The more you use the telephone, the easier it will be.

FACE-TO-FACE MARKETING: THE INTERVIEW

> Interviews are a lot like a baseball game. Just when it looks like you've caught a job offer, a curve ball comes out of nowhere and you strike out.
>
> Author Unknown

Your plight in the interview is very much like that of the Olympic runner I spoke about in Part 1. There is usually only one shot at winning. If he loses, the runner doesn't get another chance for a long time. You, on the other hand, do not get a second chance at all.

Your objective is to get the job offer. The customer is asking what you can do for his or her company. The objective is to find out why she should hire you.

Help the interviewer choose you. Think of the interview as a three-part process:

1. Pre-Interview: What happens before?
2. The Interview: What happens during?
3. Post-Interview: What happens after?

Pre-Interview: What Happens Before?

The amount of effort invested before the interview is directly related to your success in the interview itself. Preparation cannot be overlooked or done in a casual manner. Learn everything you can about the company and the interviewer. Use annual reports and directories such as Dun & Bradstreet's or Standard & Poor's. Try to identify people sources, too. Use your contacts to help you.

Research

Research helps you ask intelligent questions and respond with a thoroughness that leaves a clear and powerful impact on the interviewer. Asking questions about the company shows finesse and initiative. Some areas in which to gather data include:

- Product line
- Sales volume (for at least 5 years)
- Ownership (public or private)
- Major markets
- Credit rating
- Profitability
- Recent history
- The interviewer's history, if possible
- Company structure and organization

Cross Over . . . Again

Place yourself on the interviewer's side of the desk. What is he/she thinking? What questions will he/she ask? Write a list of questions and add them to the list of possible questions to expect. Take all the time you need. Write out the answers to every question. If you are having difficulty responding to one in particular, it's better to have it surface now so you can refine the answer.

Rehearse. Practice again and again. Role play with a friend. Be sure you feel comfortable with your answers. Make sure your responses are short and to the point, yet conversational (more about how to make the interviewer comfortable later in this section). In the interview, you may encounter the questions listed below. Be prepared to answer them. Write out the answers, then practice them on cassette and/or videotape. Reviewing your responses and your interviewing image is extremely valuable.

Interview Questions to Expect

1. Tell me what you know about us.
2. What do you find most and least attractive about the position?
3. Tell me why we should hire you.
4. What do you look for in a position?
5. What do you look for in the ideal environment?
6. Describe your management philosophy.
7. Describe your management style.
8. What do you look for in hiring others?
9. Have you ever fired anyone? If so, why? How was it handled?
10. What is the most difficult about moving from one job to another?
11. Describe the significant trends in this industry.
12. Tell me about your current employer.
13. How do your subordinates view you?
14. Tell me about your major accomplishments in your career.
15. Tell me about your major accomplishments in your current or last position.
16. Describe your boss.
17. Do you like staff or line work? Why?
18. Describe your personality.
19. What do you do in your spare time?
20. What are your short- and long-range goals?
21. What other opportunities are you considering?
22. What are you looking for in a salary?
23. How long will you be here before you make a contribution to our firm?

24. Why aren't you earning more, given your age?
25. Do you consider yourself a good manager? Why?
26. Why are you leaving your employer? (or did you leave?)
27. Tell me about your strengths and limitations.
28. About how many hours do you put in per day? Per week?
29. What did you like and dislike about your last employer?
30. Why are you interested in the job we have available?
31. Are you active in any professional associations? If so, which?
32. What do you feel motivates you most?

Presentation

Getting yourself personally ready for the interview takes thought and planning. Making a favorable first impression is the first step in successfully controlling the interview meeting.

These simple rules and reminders are common sense, but they can make the difference between success and failure—between winning and losing!

Appearance

There is only one way to dress for the interview: conservatively. It is easier for the man because the dress code has been established. He should wear a dark suit with a crisp white or blue shirt and dark polished shoes. Be well-groomed and cleanly shaven. Pay particular attention to details such as your hands. They don't have to be professionally manicured, but they must be meticulous.

For the female candidate, conservative dress is also advised, but add to it a sense of style. This can include the use of such accessories as a belt, a scarf, and jewelry. The rule is to keep it simple and conservative, but at the same time you can add a small personal touch such as a pastel blouse or a scarf. Keep your make-up light . . . it should enhance your looks without being noticeable. Your hairstyle should be neat and attractive without being flamboyant. Your hands should be well-manicured, and the color of your nailpolish should be conservative. It would be best to wear a well-fitting suit. The conservative skirt length is below the knee. Shoes should be polished and have a medium heel. The total look should be simple, never cluttered. Pay attention to every detail, including your briefcase.

The Interview: What Happens During?

> The most effective job interview establishes a mutual exchange of information between interviewer and interviewee. Both need to determine the degree of fit—the candidate's skills, needs, and values with the requirements of the position, company, and industry. To do this, one must interview at the same time one is being interviewed, evaluate as one is being evaluated, seek information as one gives it.
>
> Edward B. Rettig, Ph.D.
> Principal
> RMA Consulting
> Los Angeles-Based Outplacement Firm

The interview is an opportunity to sell yourself in person. Regardless of your level of interest, you do want this opportunity. There are two kinds of interviews: one is for a bonafide job opening; the other is for gathering information that can generate leads or contact referrals. The focus here is on selling yourself in the job interview.

In either case, you want it to be successful and positive. Interviewers generally want the meeting to be comfortable and rewarding for both of you.

▸ **Strategy 15:** Learn to make the interviewer's job easier.

How to Develop a Relationship with the Person on the Other Side of the Desk

You need to remain aware of the Cross Over Strategy throughout your job search. The "what do they want" and "what are they feeling" issues are very important in the actual interview.

- Developing good rapport is critical. Your job is to make the interviewer feel comfortable. The better he/she likes you, the better the chances for being asked to return for another interview and ultimately for getting the job offer. Be positive and relax. There are ways to help this decision maker enjoy being with you. Be confident and pleasant. Listen attentively and ask questions intelligently . . . your future depends on it.
- Watch and emulate the voice, the pace, and the style of the person on the other side of the desk. Be sure that you are not doing most of the talking. Do not argue or say too much about yourself. Above all, do not oversell.
- Keep any negative information about previous positions and companies to yourself. Even if you dislike your former company or boss, discuss these potentially negative issues in a positive way. Practice this before you arrive at the interview.
- Show energy and enthusiasm, but tailor it to the interviewer's level. A strong handshake and a straightforward "I am interested in this job" can prove beneficial.
- Tell the truth. Sometimes even an omission can grow out of proportion.
- Ask the interviewer questions that will motivate her to talk about the job, the company, and herself. Do this without appearing to control the interview. The answers will give you more power when responding to questions. Try to get her to open up early in the interview; she may answer your questions upfront. With practice, you can learn to take charge of the interview while making it appear as though the interviewer is in full control. Not every interviewer will let you get away with it. However, it is certainly worth a try. Creating a conversational atmosphere should be your underlying objective throughout the interview.

Some Suggested Questions to Ask

Use the following questions as a trigger to help you develop other questions:

1. What is the company's growth plan? for the next year? for the next five years?
2. Does the company usually promote from within?
3. Is this a replacement or a new position?
4. How long was the previous person in this position? Why is she/he no longer in the position?
5. What is the career path?
6. What is the growth potential?
7. If the interviewer is your potential supervisor, ask about his or her career experience and future career growth.

Good Business Sense Is Good Business Etiquette

Don't assume that you are a personal friend. The interview is and always will be a business relationship no matter how comfortable or enjoyable the meeting becomes.

Be respectful. This is the interviewer's territory. You NEVER have the right to argue or strongly disagree. However, being yourself is also important. You are a person. You have a right to have opinions. You don't have to be a "yes" person. However, be careful what or how much you say.

Simple common courtesies like "thank you" are expected. You are not exempt from good business etiquette of any kind.

It is perfectly acceptable to ask when you can expect a decision and to state that you would like to be able to call after the interview if you have any questions.

Post-Interview: What Happens After?

Immediately after leaving the interview, evaluate how it went. Do you sense that the interview culminated with the feeling of mutual esteem? Were you effectively communicating your abilities, experience, and strengths? Did you tend to ramble? How do you feel it went? Good? Bad? Why? What and when is the next step?

Follow-Up/Thank You Letter

Within three days of the interview, you should follow-up with a letter or telephone call. A letter is preferable. Refer to your accomplishments and experience and how they relate to the position. Include the following in your letter:

- A thank you for the interview.
- Express your interest in the position. If you are not interested, tell them so. If you are interested in the company, leave the door open in case more suitable possibilities become available.
- If you are told you are no longer a viable candidate, try to leave things open for future possibilities.
- Explain how your skills and experience fit the position.
- If an offer is extended, state your appreciation and tell them you will get back to them with an answer.

If you have not heard from the company after approximately two weeks, it is acceptable to contact the company.

Expense Reimbursement

If the company is to reimburse you for expenses incurred for coming to the interview, mail in your expense reimbursement request (no later than a week after you return home). Total all items and enclose all appropriate receipts. I have seen candidates wait until they are asked for these. This is not a good idea.

Follow-Up Self-Assessment

After the interview, consider the following questions. Write your responses. The best way to improve your interview score next time is to pay attention to the post-assessment.

1. Did you establish rapport?
2. How did you handle being nervous?
3. Were you appropriately dressed?
4. Did you point out your strengths and accomplishments?
5. Did you ask pertinent questions showing your understanding of the position?
6. Did you get enough needed information?
7. What is the next step?

Post-Interview Record

Set up a card file to record each interview. Include the following:

- Date of interview
- Interviewer
- Title
- Company
- Products
- Title of position
- Salary
- Next step (include date)
- Letter sent (date of)
- Your estimate of the interviewer's impression
- Ways to have improved the interview (include what you might have done prior to meeting)

The interview is not a dress rehearsal. It is opening night; it is the big game . . . the playoffs. Prepare yourself to get the job.

9

Sources and Resources: Look Everywhere

If a man look sharply and attentively, he shall see fortune . . .

William Shakespeare

There are many resources available to help you find the job you want. This chapter will show you what they are and where to find them. Be sure to consider all possibilities.

▸ **Strategy 16:** The more creative you are in using all available resources, the more effective you will be.

Concentrate your efforts in these four major areas:

- People: The contacts you know and those you need to know
- Advertisements and News: Advertisements and news in publications, journals, and newspapers
- Books: Business reference books, career books
- Organizations: Associations, chambers of commerce, college placement offices, executive recruiters and search firms, consulting firms, state and federal government

PEOPLE

Contacts are the most important resource for jobs, leads, and referrals. Statistics show that contacts are the most successful job-hunting tool. Some studies indicate that as many as 85 percent of the successful job candidates found their positions because of a contact. The higher you are in the organization, the more important the people are in your network.

You will want to meet your contacts for a personal interview whenever possible. They will remember you better if they know you as more than just one or two pieces of paper with your career history written on it.

There are four types of contacts:

- Personal friends
- Business associates (colleagues, subordinates, or superiors)
- Individuals who may need to be reminded that they know you
- Contacts who are referrals with whom you have never met

List all the people who come to mind. Aim for an initial list of 100 names. Perhaps you will think of a name, but cannot imagine how he can help you at this time. Ask yourself if there is any possible way that he may be of assistance in the future. If so, add his name to your list. Also, do not forget those who cannot help you, but who know someone else who can. After you complete this list, place an A or a B in the left margin beside each name.

Place an A beside each name that can most effectively lead you to a job or another good contact. Place a B beside those names that can do this less effectively or that you are unsure about. Now use this list to make two separate lists: list A and list B (see the samples on pp. 180–181).

Your contacts list will continue to grow as you obtain more referrals and more contacts.

ADVERTISEMENTS AND THE NEWS

Most job seekers rely on the classified section of the newspaper to find a job opening. You should not depend on this as a major source, because you will be competing with hundreds of job candidates who are reading the very same ad.

SAMPLE LIST A—BEST CONTACTS

Name	Company	Telephone	Date Comment	Date Follow-Up

SAMPLE LIST B—SECONDARY LIST OF CONTACTS

Name Company Telephone	Date Comment	Date Follow-Up

Many jobs have not yet been fully conceptualized. The personnel department has not yet been told about the opening; therefore, the ad has not yet been written. This is called the "Hidden Job Market" you hear so much about.

Therefore, when you use the "help wanted" ads, approach them intelligently and with a specific strategy in mind:

- Answer ads even though your background doesn't exactly match. The perfect candidate often does not exist. The ad may require a degree, skills, or experience that you do not have, but if this is a job you think you want, answer the ad anyway. Most candidates will probably not meet all of the requirements.
- Consider that you may fill the requirements of a position that would manage the position advertised.
- You may fill a position before an ad is placed.
- If this is the beginning of your job search, go back three months and clip the ads. Some appear as little as once and take months to be filled.
- An additional approach is to go back one year. Call or write to the companies that interest you. The individual who was hired may not have worked out. After researching previous ads, concentrate on the present.

Blind Ads

Responses to a blind ad, one that does not identify the employer, are sent to a box number. Most box numbers can be used for several months. Blind advertisements are a fairly good source because fewer candidates are likely to respond.

One reason a company uses a blind ad is to maintain anonymity from their own employees as well as their competition. Since you don't know who this company is, you could be sending your résumé to your own boss!

Newspapers

Newspapers are a major informational source for company and industry trends as well as for potential job openings. Use both present and back issues to help you with this research. Look for:

- Company relocations
- Company or product expansions
- Company earnings
- Management changes (new ideas and/or major expansion of personnel)
- Classified ads for company growth trends, salary information, and potential jobs

Local Newspapers

Small city and community papers generally focus on lower-level positions. However, if you are interested in a particular area, it is helpful to scan the ads and business news in the local papers of your preferred location.

Major Newspapers

The following major newspapers have ads covering positions all over the United States. The Sunday editions contain advertisements for senior-level and higher-paid positions. Subscribe to the relevant Sunday edition of the newspapers identified next:

The Atlanta Journal and
The Atlanta Constitution
P.O. Box 4689
Atlanta, GA 30302
(404) 526-5151

Chicago Tribune
435 North Michigan Avenue
Chicago, IL 60611
(312) 222-4100

Los Angeles Times
P.O. Box 60164
Los Angeles, CA 90060
(213) 626-2323

San Francisco Examiner and Chronicle
925 Mission Street
San Francisco, CA 94103
(415) 777-7000

New York Times
229 West 43rd Street
New York, NY 10036
(212) 556-7292

Washington Post
1150 15th Street N.W.
Washington, DC 20071
(202) 334-6100

The Wall Street Journal is the best resource for middle and upper management openings. It is published in four regional editions: Western, Southwestern, Midwestern, and Eastern. On Tuesday, you will find the largest selection of ads. Subscribe to the regional edition that most interests you.

The Wall Street Journal
200 Burnett Road
Chicopee, MA 01021
(413) 592-7761

A second *Wall Street Journal* source is the *National Business Employment Weekly*. It is a compilation of the weekly *Wall Street Journal* regional want ads. Contact:

National Business Employment Weekly
420 Lexington Avenue
New York, NY 10170
(212) 808-6792

The following two publications are similar to the *National Business Employment Weekly* in that they both carry advertisements from around the country. However, the *National AdSearch* and *Jobweek* service numerous newspapers in major cities, while the *National Business Employment Weekly* relies solely on the regional *Wall Street Journal* papers. The *National AdSearch* and *Jobweek* are published weekly and bi-monthly, respectively. Contact:

The National AdSearch
P.O. Box 2083
Milwaukee, WI 53201
(414) 351-1398

Jobweek, Inc.
307 W. Main Street
Fredericksburg, TX 98624
(512) 997-8877

Association Publications and Trade Journals

Nearly every industry or business has a trade association. Association magazines and newsletters often have classified listings of job opportunities. The potential assistance—information, as well as contacts through the membership lists—is worth your consideration.

Trade associations often have membership directories that are available to members. If you can gain access to a directory, you may be able to contact members by mail and/or telephone. One senior financial executive sent everyone in the local 260-member roster his résumé. As a result, he was given four interviews for actual job openings. Most associations also have job referral services that put job seekers in touch with employers. *The Encyclopedia of Associations* is the authoritative source in identifying the most appropriate associations for the position you seek.

In addition to trade association directories, the following publications may be helpful:

> *Guide to Professional Organizations*
> The Carroll Press, Inc.
> In this excellent resource there are nearly 2000 listings of organizations by field.
>
> *National Trade and Professional Associations of the U.S. and Canada and Labor Unions*
> Columbia Books, Inc.
> Six thousand listings, includes labor unions, technical societies, trade associations, and more; organized by key word and by executive director, geographically and alphabetically.

All the information you need is available to you. To find it, you need to have perserverence, time, and patience.

Targeted Direct Mail

(A targeted mailing list that is compiled by you to mail to potential employers) This is an effective way to reach the unadvertised jobs in the hidden market mentioned above. Use the following recommendations:

- Use the research sources in the Business Reference Books list (p. 187 to locate the list of target companies that interest you).
- Be sure to address your letter to the name and title of the individual who is the decision maker.
- For the name of the key individual, use the directories suggested in the book list that follows. If possible, call the company and ask the name and correct title of the executive.
- The broadcast letter may be more appropriate for your direct mail campaign. However, if your résumé fits the position you

are seeking in a particular organization, then a cover letter and résumé is preferred.

- Use caution. Although you could send hundreds of letters out intermittently, it has been demonstrated that the larger the number of letters you mail to the marketplace, the less effective is your campaign.

BOOKS

Business Reference Books

This list is vital to researching various companies. After you have established your position objective(s), you then need to identify the target companies and the name and title of the person with the authority to hire you. The following list of books will assist you with this research.

The Business Reference Librarian, in most major libraries, can assist you in locating and using these reference sources. This is not a complete listing, nor is there a complete directory. Some books indicate the size of the company, while others tell who the parent organization is. This list should contain all the information you will need; if not, ask the reference librarian for further assistance.

Business Organizations and Agencies Directory
(specialized organizations and agencies, both United States and foreign)

Business Periodicals Index
(published monthly, commonly available up to 10 years back, a subject index to articles in business magazines)

Dictionary of Occupational Titles (D.O.T.)
U.S. Department of Labor

Directory of Corporate Affiliations
(Who Owns Whom)

Directory of Directories
(two volume list of published directories)

Directory of European Industrial & Trade Associations
(companies located in Europe)

Directory of European Associations Part 2
(Professional Associations)

Directory of Manufacturers in the United States

Electronic News Financial Fact Book & Directory

Encyclopedia of Associations,
4 volumes

Encyclopedia of Business Information Sources
(directories, journals/periodicals, companies, source books, and bibliographies)

Guide to American Directories
(specialized directories)

International Directory of Corporate Affiliations
(who owns whom worldwide)

Million Dollar Directory Series
(160,000 plus, both public and private companies. 5 volumes, Dun & Bradstreet)

Moody's Manuals
(financial statements, company rating by sales volume and profit margin, officers in publicly held companies)

Occupational Outlook Handbook
Department of Labor (forecasts)

Reference Book of Corporate Managements
(biographical profiles of principal officers and directors in 12,000 plus leading U.S. companies, 4 volumes, Dun & Bradstreet)

Standard Directory of Advertisers
(two editions, (1) classified—arranged by product and (2) geographical—arranged by state and city.)

Standard & Poor's Register of Corporations, Directors, and Executives
Vol. 1: over 45,000 corporations, officers, sales volume, number of employees
Vol. 2: directors and officers, nearly 70,000 listings
Vol. 3: lists companies by S.I.C. number, geographic location, and corporate families

Thomas Register of American Manufacturers
(by product and trade name, but no officers)

Ulrich's International Periodicals
(trade periodicals)

Yellow Pages
(good source locally as well as in other states)

ORGANIZATIONS

There are many organizations in which you will find both personal contacts and written resources. The first place to look is within your own professional associations. Start there, and then use every other available organization that you can find. Even unrelated community organizations are viable sources of referral information and leads.

Associations

Start with the *Encyclopedia of Associations* to identify all the professional associations in your field. Contact those that are the more closely linked to your industry and function. These associations will provide you with an abundance of job information. The publications have advertisements for actual jobs, and the membership directories are excellent for contact development. In addition, many associations have an employment service.

Chambers of Commerce

Most states and major cities have a directory of businesses and industries published by the state or city Chamber of Commerce. These directories are a good place to start if you are interested in a particular geographic location.

Overseas Chambers of Commerce, Foreign Embassies, and American Embassies

This advice will be helpful if your interest is in an American company in a foreign country, a foreign company with an American subsidiary, or a foreign company overseas.

- Go to your local Chamber of Commerce to locate the address of a foreign Chamber of Commerce.
- Addresses for American Embassies and foreign Chambers of Commerce are in the directory entitled *Worldwide Chamber of Commerce Directory*.
- If you are in a major city such as Chicago, use the white pages of the telephone book to locate phone numbers and addresses of the Foreign Embassies (Consulates) you are interested in. If this is not a possible information source for you, call Directory Assistance, Washington, DC, (202) 555-1212 for Foreign Embassy listings.

College Placement Offices and Publications

Many college placement offices, particularly in the graduate business schools, provide lists of job openings, as well as a registration service, to applicants. Try the college you attended and the colleges or universities in the area in which you are interested. Determine whether the services and publications of these placement offices can be of assistance to you.

Executive Recruiters (Contingency)

Contingency firms generally serve lower and sometimes middle-level management ($25,000 to $75,000 range plus). They are an important source, particularly if the firm specializes in your function or industry. This is not a place for career counseling. The fees are paid by the employer after you begin work. As the salary range indicates, this is a good source for mid- and nonmanagement candidates.

Executive Search Firms (Retainer)

An executive search firm is retained by the employer to search for high-level people to fill specific employer needs and requirements. If you have middle to senior management salary requirements, skills, and experiences, an executive search firm is an excellent place to send your résumé and cover letter. The minimum salary is usually $50,000 or more.

If you want a national listing of Executive Recruiters of both the Contingency and Search firms, an excellent source is: *Directory of Executive Recruiters,* Consultants News, Inc. Templeton Rd., Fitzwilliam, NH 03447.

Consulting Firms

See *Consultants and Consultant Organizations,* First Edition by Paul Wasserman and Willis R. Greer, Jr., Graduate School of Business and Public Administration, Cornell University, Ithaca, New York. This directory contains listings (by state, specialization, and alphabetical order) of firms that consult to businesses.

State or Federal Government

You will find the same kinds of jobs here as in the private sector. For entry level jobs, a test is generally given.

State Employment Service

There is a free list of available jobs at your local State Employment Office. These jobs have lower skill and salary requirements. For management and senior-level executive positions, this is a highly unlikely source.

10

Where to Go for Help

Now is no time to think of what you do not have. Think of what you can do with what there is.

Ernest Hemingway

Scenario One:
For whatever reason, John Mason is at a deadend in his job search (or at least that is the way he feels right now).

Scenario Two:
Corinne Carson has been searching on her own for quite awhile, but she hasn't found a job yet. She has been the number two candidate more than once, and is beginning to get frustrated and discouraged.

Scenario Three:
Jerry Rollins is a part of the senior management team in his company. An acquisition will be completed within 30 days. Not only will he be out of a job, but there will be no outplacement provided for anyone.

The only thing all of these people have in common is that they need help.

▶ **Strategy 17:** It is foolish to try to conduct a job search without professional guidance.

What can they do? There is more than one option available. Some are better than others. The following is a brief review of the sources. If you need help, refer to these options and decide which would be best for you.

Do It Yourself

Though this is the hard way, there is an honesty about it because you now know you must take on the responsibility for your own job search. There is no way to place blame elsewhere or to wait for someone else to do it. This means relying on the How-To Books (found in the libraries and bookstores) and the advice of friends and family. You can't beat the upfront cost, and you would probably be seeking their advice anyway. The difference is that you are now dependent on their counsel—good or bad. If your job search takes a long time, this kind of assistance becomes very costly, because poor advice is always costly. However, friends and family can be helpful in the building of a strong and effective network. Finding a job without any outside help is difficult; it is nearly impossible to be totally objective about one's own job search. Other negative aspects of doing it yourself is that it is time consuming and usually not as effective.

If you are on your own, this book was written so that you can do it yourself more easily and effectively. You are now equipped with all the latest and best knowledge you need to write a winning résumé, to have a successful interview, to know your objectives, and to build a solid network of contacts and referrals. You also know where to get information about the companies you are interested in. You will not be deterred for lack of knowledge; therefore, you will win the job-search game.

College Career Counseling Centers

These counseling offices offer career counseling, sometimes for a nominal fee, to nonstudents. Check out the business acumen of the counselor. It could be a good resource.

Agencies with Sliding-Fee Scales

Usually, these are nonprofit organizations. Many of the church-sponsored groups, such as Catholic Charities and Jewish Vocational Services, have rather extensive programs. Your own clergy may be a good place to start. Many high-level people have gone through some of these agency programs.

Career Counselors

There are almost as many career counselors as there are job seekers. Some offer testing, some charge by the hour, others work at home, some see people in the suburbs, others only have office hours during the day, some have a Ph.D., others have an M.S.W. or other graduate degree. Of course, there are those with no credentials at all. Some are excellent. Others are unscrupulous. Still others are merely ineffective.

A good counselor can help you package yourself and develop a marketing strategy. Be smart and ask questions about their experiences and their references. There are two types of counselors: one shows you how to proceed and points you in the right direction. This counselor might work with you for as little as one hour, but would be there when you need help.

The other prefers the long-term support relationship. He will meet with you each week until you find a job. Both types of career counseling are viable. It depends on what you need and how much you want to spend.

Fees are either at a fixed rate or by the hour. Hourly fees are in the $35 to $125 range. Flat fee programs offer a set number of hours or a specified program for fees of $400 to $1200 plus.

Résumé Service

Using a résumé service is an excellent way to get your résumé stored on a computer disk for future edits. Furthermore, your letters and envelopes can be done cost-effectively. Unless you have the resources to do this on your own in a clear, crisp, and professional manner, a résumé service is worth considering.

Be cautious about the résumé service that offers career counseling. Unless such a firm has the expertise and the credentials, their advice could stall or extend your job search. There are, however, services like The Résumé Store, a Chicago based résumé service, that offers personalized and professional service. The proprietors are good at what they do because they do not pretend to be career counselors. There are other such firms in your city. To find them, investigate and ask for references.

Outplacement Firms

There are two very different kinds of outplacement firms:

The Retail Outplacement Firm

This type of firm accepts fees from individuals. These firms use large newspaper display ads to advertise their services. They promise to help executives find jobs. Some have been known to make guarantees about contacts and finding jobs for their clients. The fees they charge are high. They ask clients to sign a legally binding contract. Don't be surprised if they offer to help obtain a loan for you.

The Executive Outplacement Firm

On the other hand, the executive outplacement firm receives its fees from employers. They are retained by a corporation to work on behalf of its displaced employees to assist them through successful career transitions. Executive outplacement is an excellent idea. Ask for it; your company just may give it to you. Be wary of any firm that doesn't care whether the fee comes from you or the company. An executive outplacement firm does not accept a fee from an individual. At the first screening, this fee could be your only clue. Look further for the differences, because they are there. For example, executive outplacement firms generally do not guarantee that they will "place" their clients.

Job Search Support Group

This is one of the best sources of help. You can put a group together on your own. Job seekers, as well as people who are trying to improve their positions, gain immeasurable help from each other. Meet regularly—at least twice a month. Assign different members to take turns in the leadership. Limit the group to 10 members. The occupations and professions can be varied. However, the commitment and sense of generosity of each group member needs to be similar. Build a structure for managing confidentiality. Each group member should have 10 minutes to share his situation and to take notes on what the group recommends. Set up a buddy system to keep each other going between meetings.

Group support is highly recommended. This help knows no boundaries. There isn't any executive manager or professional who wouldn't benefit from such a group. If you cannot find one to join, start your own.

Career Guide Books

See the Bibliography for a list of books on assessment, internal career management, interviewing techniques, job search strategies, and résumé development. This list is by no means complete, since new books appear with some regularity as older ones become dated. For other help, see the business and career sections in your local library and in the book stores.

If you decide to seek help from any of the above sources, be sure to check out their services and their references thoroughly. If you have any doubts, call your local District Attorney or the State's Attorney. This is a critical decision; investigate before you buy.

Appendix
Survey Methodology

WHO WAS SELECTED

The job market for executives is the totality of CEOs, other senior officers, corporate recruiters, executive recruiters, and other such people. All were selected for this research study on the assumption that they make decisions about the future of each executive résumé that lands on their desk.

The survey covered a cross-section of firms and decision makers across the country.

Four different groups of résumé readers were included.

1. CEOs and senior officers were selected at random from a variety of business and association directories.
2. Employment managers were chosen at random from directories.
3. Personnel and human resource generalists were identified from association membership lists.
4. Executive search and contingency firms were selected from association rosters.
5. Executive outplacement consultants were geographically selected.

HOW IT WAS DONE

The survey was done in three ways:

1. Face-to-face interviews
2. A mailing to a pilot population to solicit comments and further refine the survey
3. Another mailing to a broader population to gather data

This methodology provided the opportunity to look at the data from a variety of perspectives and to draw more valid assumptions.

WHO RESPONDED

A total of 394 surveys were mailed to a cross section of organizations and various decision makers. Not only were 132 returned; comments and phone calls were received that said, in effect, "This was an important subject . . . very needed and timely." A 34 percent return validates those comments and the assumption that new research on what employers really want in a résumé was a worthwhile effort. However, I was surprised at the high level of response and interest in what (on the surface) could be described as a dry subject—the résumé.

In addition, the staff of Cambridge Human Research Group personally interviewed 31 decision makers to further clarify the appropriate questions and to gather more data. A total of 163 individuals were surveyed.

The respondents were from six types of organizations:

Corporations (the majority of responses—80 percent)
Hospitals/Healthcare
Academic/Government
CPA/Consulting Firms

Executive Recruiting Firms
Outplacement Firms

The titles of these decisions makers included:

President
Managing Partner
Partner
General Manager
Executive Vice President
Senior Vice President
Vice President
Director
Manager
Employment Representative
Other

Over 38 percent of those responding were at the manager level. Director level was the second largest population to respond to the survey (31 percent). Twelve percent at the top of the house (CEO, COO, Senior VP, etc.) took the time to respond to the survey themselves.

The diverse range of industries are ranked below by the number of respondents. The top four industry categories make up nearly 65 percent of the respondents.

High Tech (Computers, Communications, Electronics)
Banking
Food/Beverage
Healthcare/Pharmaceuticals
Other Consumer Products
Other Manufacturing
Retail

Oil/Gas
Forest Products/Packaging
Publishing
Advertising/Marketing/Public Relations
Management Consulting Firms

As many as 63 percent of those surveyed see over 500 résumés a year. Less than 1 percent see under 25. Another 29 percent see between 100 to 500 résumés. The survey seems to be a fair representation of résumé decision makers. These people see a large number of résumés and, hence, are experienced in culling out. The knock-you-out skill is finely honed.

Although 33 percent of those surveyed are responsible for hiring salaries up to $50,000, these people also seem to be making the you're-in-or-you're-out decisions for more senior level candidates. Under 25 percent of the respondents have primary responsibility for recruiting candidates earning over $100,000.

Bibliography

ASSESSMENT

Hapberg, Janet, and Richard Leider. *The Inventurers, Excursions in Life and Career Renewal.* Reading, MA: Addison-Wesley, 1982.

Jackson, Tom. *How to Get the Job You Want in 28 Days.* New York: Dutton, 1977.

Sher, Barbara, and Annie Gottlieb. *Wishcraft.* New York: Ballantine Books, 1979.

CAREER MANAGEMENT

Houze, William C. *Career Veer.* New York: McGraw Hill, 1985.

McCormack, Mark H. *What They Don't Teach You at Harvard Business School.* Toronto: Bantam Books, 1984.

Tarrant, John. *Stalking the Headhunter.* New York: Bantam Books, 1986.

INTERVIEWING

Faux, Marian. *The Executive Interview.* New York: St. Martin's Press, 1985.

Krannich, Caryl Rae. *Interview for Success.* Virginia Beach, VA: Impact Publications,

Medley, H. Anthony. *Sweaty Palms: The Neglected Art of Being Interviewed.* Belmont, CA: Lifetime Learning Publications, 1978.

JOB SEARCH STRATEGY

Birsner, Patricia E. *Job Hunting for the 40+ Executive.* New York: Facts on File Publications, 1985.

Cohen, William A. *The Executive's Guide to Finding a Superior Job.* New York: American Management Association, 1978.

DeRoche, Frederick W., and Mary A. McDougall. *Now It's Your Move.* Englewood Cliffs, NJ: Prentice-Hall, 1984.

Jackson, Tom. *Guerrilla Tactics in the Job Market.* Toronto: Bantam Books, 1978.

Myers, Albert M., and Christopher P. Anderson. *Success Over Sixty.* New York: Summit Books, 1984.

Payne, Richard A. *How To Get a Better Job Quicker.* New York: New American Library, 1972.

Stanat, Kirby W., and Patrick Reardon. *Job Hunting Secrets and Tactics.* Milwaukee, WI: Westwind Press, 1977.

RÉSUMÉ WRITING

Beatty, Richard H. *The Résumé Kit.* New York: Wiley, 1984.

Bostwick, Burdette E. *Résumé Writing.* New York: Wiley, 1985.

Bruce, Stephen D. Ph.D. *Writing Résumés.* Madison, CT: Business and Legal Reports, 1985.

Foxman, Loretta D. *Résumés That Work, How To Sell Yourself on Paper.* New York: Wiley, 1984.

Hochneiser, Robert. *Throw Away Your Résumé!* Woodbury, NY: Barron's Educational Series, 1982.

Jackson, Tom. *The Perfect Résumé.* Garden City, NY: Anchor Press/Doubleday, 1981.

Kennedy, Marilyn Moats. *Writing Résumés That Sell.* Wilmette, IL: Career Strategies, 1983.

Schuman, Nancy, and William Lewis. *Revising Your Résumé.* New York: Wiley, 1986.

Index